Heart of the Rock

HEART OF THE ROCK

THE INDIAN INVASION OF ALCATRAZ

■

by Adam Fortunate Eagle
In Collaboration with Tim Findley
Foreword by Vine Deloria, Jr.

Photographs by Vincent Maggiora, Brooks Townes, and Ilka Hartmann

Photoediting by Ilka Hartmann

University of Oklahoma Press : Norman

Library of Congress Cataloging-in-Publication Data

Fortunate Eagle, Adam
Heart of the Rock: the Indian invasion of Alcatraz /
by Adam Fortunate Eagle in collaboration with Tim
Findley; foreword by Vine Deloria, Jr.; photographs
by Vincent Maggiora, Brooks Townes,
and Ilka Hartmann.
p.   cm.
ISBN 978-0-8061-3369-6 (cloth)
ISBN 978-0-8061-3989-0 (paper)
1. Alcatraz Island (Calif.)—History—Indian occupation, 1969–1971.
2. Indians of North America—Government relations.
3. Indians of North America—Urban residence.
4. Indians of North America—Ethnic identity.
I. Findley, Tim.
II. Title
E78.C15 E16 2002
979.4′61—dc21
2001048071

The paper in this book meets the guidelines for perma-
nence and durability of the Committee on Production
Guidelines for Book Longevity of the Council on
Library Resources, Inc. ∞

2 3 4 5 6 7 8 9 10

Contents

Illustrations

foreword

IF ANYONE CAN TELL THE STORY OF ALCATRAZ from start to finish, it is Adam Fortunate Eagle, who was here, there, and everywhere in the Bay Area during the turbulent sixties. I first met Adam at the Capitol Conference on Poverty in Washington, D.C., in May 1964. Gathered at the National Cathedral were some four hundred Indians hoping to get ourselves special mention in the pending Economic Opportunity Act—the "War on Poverty." Adam began talking about Indian problems in the Bay Area in the cash bar about 9 P.M. and concluded around 2 A.M., at which point the man running the cash bar gave him the evening's receipts to solve Indian poverty and left the room with tears in his eyes.

While I was director of the National Congress of American Indians (NCAI), Adam would keep me informed on Bay Area activities and often talked about getting Alcatraz back from the government. In late October 1969 we had a conference in San Francisco to find a way to bring urban Indian centers into the NCAI as regular voting members, and following the meeting a fire broke out at the Indian Center rendering it useless for further programs. Within a few days Adam was on the phone telling me that an invasion was imminent, and when the first brief encounter was followed by the real occupation we all waited tensely to see if the marshals were going to remove everyone. I suspect the Proclamation saved the day because of its irony—Indians wanting the Rock because it had no more resources and services than the average reservation.

The world press focused on the occupation and suddenly it was necessary to have some kind of plan, assuming that the Rock would be handed over. Alcatraz helped to highlight existing struggles that were occurring elsewhere and the Indians began to steal the spotlight from other issues. Unfortunately, most stories were written in the old frontier lingo—"Indian

Uprising," and so forth—so that while there were many issues to raise regarding Indians, it was very difficult to get some serious reporting done. By Christmas, interest was starting to fade and on Christmas Eve Adam convinced me to go to Alcatraz and talk with the occupants to formulate some kind of program that would get Alcatraz back in the news. But there was tremendous factionalism on the Rock and our meeting accomplished very little except to harden the stances of the conflicting parties.

In late January I convinced Merv Griffin to tape a segment of his show on the Rock and he devoted considerable time on one of his evening talk shows to Alcatraz. My memories now become blurred because a number of us made endless trips to Alcatraz to suggest ways to get the administration seriously interested in giving back the island, but changing constituency on Alcatraz made it impossible to keep anything on the agenda. Various movie stars and rock bands made the obligatory visit to encourage the occupants, but sometimes these visits convinced the occupiers to simply enjoy the publicity. The group had called themselves "Indians of All Tribes" and soon the name caught on in other parts of the country. Bernie Whitebear and his ally, Jane Fonda, invaded Fort Lawton near Seattle, designating themselves by the same name.

The Rock did symbolize the revival of Indians as real people to a generation of young Indians across the country. Hundreds, perhaps thousands, of Indians flocked to the Bay Area to be THERE—where things were happening. In many respects it was equivalent to the hippie–Woodstock nation ideology that brought young white kids to San Francisco in 1967. There was a tremendous amount of positive Indian energy there but no social or political framework in which it could be channeled. Richard Oakes was killed in northern California and that seemed to dampen efforts across the country, although sporadic protests continued.

During the occupation some Indian students on the East Coast planned an ill-fated invasion of Ellis Island in New York Harbor. They had plenty of press but were never able to get their outboard motors started. When queried about the plan, one student remarked that it was a pincers movement—controlling the two largest harbors in the United States would surround the white eyes.

Eventually the few remaining Indians on the island were taken off and Alcatraz became history. Adam, of course, remained at his post, changing nametags, calling meetings, guiding visitors, and negotiating with various groups in an effort to salvage something from the event.

When I read the stories of so many people of the generation after me and realize how much that experience meant to them, I also understand how small Indian affairs were in those days and how much progress we have made. The present generation has accomplished things we could not have dreamed possible. Even by the time of Wounded Knee in 1973 we had barely touched the surface of what was possible. The memory that remains with me is that wonderful feeling of freedom when you landed on the Rock. Everyday problems were swept away with the realization that we could do anything if we got together and did it.

This magnum opus by Adam is certainly one of the major stories to come from those days. It is good that he has penned this memoir before his memories fade. It will bring back those wonderful days when we were young.

VINE DELORIA, JR.

Seated: Tim Findley; *Left:* Adam Fortunate Eagle; *Right:* Walter Old Elk (naming uncle) and Marilyn Findley (Tim's wife). San Leandro, California, 1971. Annual powwow of United Bay Area Council of American Indians. Photograph courtesy of Tim Findley.

Preface

FOR HIS HELP in bringing together this book, and in providing insights into events where I could not be present, I am grateful to *Biche dakuum kukshish,* adopted son of the Whistling Water Clan, Crow Nation, who in his former life earned some recognition as the reporter Tim Findley.

I dedicate this book to Richard Oakes, who founded his tribal identity on Alcatraz and who later paid the ultimate price in fighting for the Indian cause.

I am thankful to the hundreds and then thousands, both Indian and non-Indian, who helped create a movement, the positive effects of which we still enjoy today.

Heart of the Rock

1

Turtle Island

I GUESS I AM AN OLD MAN NOW. At least these seventy-two years on my body would say I must be old. Even so, it seems to me that I will ride the back of this turtle for at least a few more years before I really feel like a senior citizen. It's an Ojibwa legend that the earth is a Turtle Island on a great lake. I like that, and I like it that younger people of my tribe today insist on the old term, "Ojibwa," instead of the anglicized "Chippewa" I used to call myself.

Turtle Island is one of those creation stories that anthropologists and missionaries love to compare among tribes, as if there is some hidden secret in them that binds together all people from the beginning of time. Maybe they are on to something.

In our case it was a great flood, a rising of the waters, that left all creatures adrift together on a log raft. A "Water World" that was better than the movies. Everywhere was water, along every horizon, without even so much as a mountain peak rising above it. The creatures became desperate in their search for land, and each of them tried in their own way to find it. Eagle soared up on the wind currents and looked far beyond where others could see, but there was nothing to be seen except water. Loon said he would find it beneath the surface where it had always been before. But even with the deep breath he took before diving in like an arrow, Loon could not see any bottom at all.

It was Muskrat who volunteered next. He could stay under much longer than Loon and swim as deep as to where it might be. The other creatures waited and waited. It was much too long even for Muskrat to be under the water, and they all feared that he must have drowned. Just then he popped back up to the surface and slowly rolled over on his back. They could see that Muskrat had made a valiant try, but it was too much for him. Together the other creatures brought poor Muskrat's body on to the raft and began to mourn for him. But Rabbit noticed that Muskrat's tiny fists were clenched on his stomach and that they were holding something. It was earth! Strong good soil that Muskrat must have found in a place too deep even for him.

"Put it on my back," said Turtle, "and we will grow from it." And so the earth began again on the back of Turtle Island.

My youngest daughter, Asha, listened through most of this story until she saw her little niece, Mishon, coming in from playing.

"I've got to go to the kitchen for a minute, Dad," she said. "Mishon, you listen to Grandpa. He's telling a story."

That's what you get when you're my age. Surrogate listeners.

There's even one member of my family who teases me all the time about telling "more damn Indian stories." I tell them anyway, just as our people have always done. It's a grandpa's privilege. That doesn't make me old, even if it does help establish me as an elder. I still work for hours every day in my shop, sculpting the artwork that pays our way. Other times, when my wife, Bobbie, and I are not traveling to some show or speaking engagement, I build on the earth lodge I am constructing from old tires and wooden beams the size of telephone poles. What "old" man still does that?

Now and then I look at one of those pictures of me from the past, me with my barbershop haircut, and even one when I'm wearing a tie and a suit. "Handsome dude," I think, "looks sort of like some movie star or politician." But was that really me? My braids have been twisted in gray and silver for many years now. I'm not certain I even have that one suit anymore, let alone have any use for it. It served its purpose, but the picture doesn't tell the story.

Bobbie and I have eleven grandchildren now, and just recently had our first great-grandchild. Our oldest grandchild, Asha's daughter, is nearly thirty and very successful where she lives in Seattle. We were so proud to give her her name when she was born: Benayshe-ba-equay, which is a combining of both our native languages—"benayshe" in Chippewa for bird, "ba" in Shoshone for water, and "equay" in Chippewa again for woman. Bird of the water woman.

Everyone calls her "Benay," and I'm not sure if she is still too shy about it to explain when people ask what it means. What it really refers to is the graceful, soaring flight of a bird that can carry away the imagination. A bird like the pelican, which in Spanish is "alcatraz."

It has been all that time of Benay's young life since Alcatraz so firmly held my full attention. At the time I wasn't much older than she is now, and as I remember it, there were so many others much younger than myself.

Blessing Ceremony, Pacific High School, San Leandro, California, ca. 1972. *Left to right:* Wilson Harrison (seated) and (standing) Adam Nordwall and Juanita Jackson. Photograph by Peter Blos, courtesy of author.

Sometimes it seems to me that you don't really get older at all, you just find an age that suits you best and live with that. I was at about that age in 1969. That point in time seems to me like a center from which I can measure all fore and since. A place of laughter and great courage, and a place of suffering and foolish mistakes.

At the time, anthropologist Margaret Mead called the Alcatraz occupation "a magnificent piece of dramatization." Lehman Brightman, a Native American Studies instructor at Berkeley who was never particularly fond of me, called it "the most important event since we actually stopped warfare with white men in 1889." But that was before either of them, or I, could see how really important and meaningful it was.

I will now take you with me on the journey that is always a circle. It's a journey of Turtle Island.

2

"If You Want It"

IT SEEMS TO ME THAT ALMOST EVERY TIME we invaded Alcatraz, some federal official was there to greet us with a memorable one-liner.

The first time, it was a befuddled-looking man who roared up to the dock in a pickup truck and identified himself as A. L. Aylworth, acting warden. In firmly polite terms he advised us that we were trespassing on federal property and should leave.

At that the attorney representing the American Indian Council, Elliott Leighton, popped open his briefcase and began reading from a sheaf of papers explaining the basis of Sioux claims to surplus federal property under terms of the 1868 Black Hills Treaty.

Aylworth listened, then scratched his head for a tense couple of seconds.

"Well," he said finally, "I guess if you want it, you can have it."

That was on a Sunday afternoon, March 8, 1964, barely a year after the last federal prisoner had been taken off the island. His name was Frank Weatherman, and he was reported to have said, as he turned his head and glared back on "the Rock" for the last time, "This place ain't never been no good for nobody."[1]

Aylworth must have thought something of the same thing as he surveyed the crowd of some forty Indians, many in full regalia, and their lawyer, all standing before him.[2]

Who in their right mind would actually want the place? Especially among an unbelievable assortment of actual Indians who looked as if they had just stepped out of some ephemeral costume documentary? I was a bit player in that day's affair, there with most of the others and a select batch of media to watch and lend support to the action of five Dakota Sioux led by Allen Cottier in staking a serious claim of their own to property the U.S. government publicly said they could find no use for.

Cottier, known among us as "Chalk," and to others by his Sioux name, "Whistler," was the most popular leader among the loosely organized Sioux Club in the Bay Area at the time, and thus our official spokesman. But history should record that it was really the inspiration and dogged determination of Richard McKenzie which led to that first "invasion." It's McKenzie, a Sioux from Rosebud, South Dakota, who should be remembered, if not as the ultimate "father" of Indian Alcatraz, then certainly as the grumpy uncle of its motivation.

Like many in the strong warrior tradition of his tribe, Dick McKenzie was a large, imposing man. He was a welder by trade, given sometimes to intimidating others as a way of making himself heard. If you argued with Dick at all, it was always best to be sure you had somebody else on your side. His threats were not so much physical, although he was capable of that. Disagreement with Dick could result in a numbing glare of derision and contempt from the Sioux leader, a look that was meant to leave his adversary feeling shunned and alone. He and I were never good friends and, later, it would come down to just such a contest of wills between us over the direction that should be taken by the United Bay Area Council of American Indians. But there is no doubt that it was McKenzie's strong presence and his personal convictions about his own tribe's treaty rights that brought the attention of us all to Alcatraz. The Sioux Club had discussed Alcatraz among themselves for weeks after the Kennedy administration first announced in 1963 that some new use would be sought for the grim icon of repression that it had become.

There is no doubt that long before San Francisco attorney Leighton was consulted for advice, and even before any of the rest of us were included for moral support, the key ideas for an occupation were formed in living room and kitchen meetings of the Sioux Club. Partly for reasons presented by the Black Hills Treaty itself, perhaps the most important Indians in that process were never given the recognition they deserve. They included Cottier's wife, Belva, along with another Dakota woman, Stella Leach, and Joan Boardman, a white woman who provided some early research, all of whom were essential to the planning. Still, it was McKenzie who seemed to forge them together, almost as if he had welded them himself from the intense smelter of his personal fire.

The 1868 treaty with the Sioux and the Arapaho aligned with Red Cloud failed to prevent intrusion into the Black Hills by white squatters and gold prospectors and led, indirectly, to the defeat of Custer at the Little Big Horn in 1876. But the treaty also contained elements describing rights for Red Cloud's people that remain in dispute today.

Article 6 of the treaty said in part: "And it is further stipulated that any male Indians, over eighteen years of age, of any band or tribe that is or who shall hereafter become a party to this treaty, who now is or shall hereafter become a resident or occupant of any reservation or territory not included in the tract of country designated . . . which is not mineral land, nor reserved by the United States for any special purposes other than Indian occupation . . . shall be entitled to receive from the United States a patent" on the land. The treaty contained some stipulations for improvements and some twists and turns, but it could be taken to mean that if the government didn't want the land, the Sioux could have it.[3]

Aylworth listened to the lawyer making all those points as if he were listening to a process server before a tax sale. Then he just decided to stand aside and let whatever was going to happen, happen.

Cottier and McKenzie were both outfitted in powerful full head-dresses of eagle feathers. McKenzie, the bigger man and dominant as ever, wore his with a simple white shirt and slacks. Cottier and a couple of younger Dakotas were more completely fitted in dance outfits down to their moccasins. But it was the full bonnets of Cottier, McKenzie, and Walter Means that drew attention and signaled a kind of authority even white people can recognize immediately. Not threatening, but confident, sure of themselves. All of them were in their early forties, but they had a bearing, a sense about them that suggested experience and standing. McKenzie carried a large American flag on a short pole that pressed across his powerful frame in flag-snapping gusts. Some of the women were wrapped in shawls or blankets that shielded them, cocoon-like, against the sea chill. It all combined to create a dramatic scene that had stepped apart from time, as the Dakota men began walking up the steep hill with the rest of us trailing after them.

Chalk, a descendant of Crazy Horse himself, blazed with a fire of his own in the cause, and his demeanor was always more flashy than McKenzie's smoldering cauldron. Aware of the attention he was drawing from the press and the photographers, Chalk braced himself against the breeze, the feathers in his bonnet slanting across his head as if blown by the speed of a charging pony.

"We'll be more fair to the government than they were to us," he said, establishing his written claim with a deerhide parchment he attached in the crevices of some rocks. "We'll pay them forty-seven cents an acre, same as they paid California tribes when the government took their land." Generously, he also offered to keep the lighthouse running, so long as it didn't interfere with other uses.

McKenzie, as always, was less eloquent and clearly more seriously determined as he solemnly set out for his own patch of priceless view amid the wild geraniums and ice plant that flooded down the hillside on the bleak and otherwise colorless twelve-acre island.

Walter Means, another much-respected Sioux, had brought along his oldest son, twenty-six-year-old Russell. Together they hammered in an old mop handle as a marker. Looking up from the hillside at the sinister mass of the old grey stone cellblock above them, Russell shook his head and said, "We'll have to tear that eyesore down." Less than a decade later Russell, as one of the leading militants of the American Indian Movement (AIM), would make a far more serious challenge to federal authorities, including heavily armed FBI agents, at a place more than a thousand miles away, Wounded Knee.

In perhaps the most theatrical, if less historically accurate, gesture, Tom Brown, another Sioux, climbed atop the stone railing at the crest of the hill carrying a polished tin tray about three feet in diameter, which he then used as a signal mirror to flash to the mainland our success—three glints for victory. There was, of course, none of our crowd left on the mainland, but the gesture was impressive.

"Acting Warden" Aylworth apparently got over his case of confusion fairly quickly. While we were on the hillside staking out individual Dakota claims and preparing for a general victory dance of our own, Aylworth was on the phone calling his boss, a real warden with hard-time experience named Richard Willard, at Willard's home in Concord. "They got beads and feathers, and everything," Aylworth was later reported to have told his annoyed boss.

When the prison was closed a year earlier, Willard had been promoted from associate warden to the unclear mission of "chief caretaker." He stomped off from a fast boat toward us, just as we had finished setting up a green camp tent that was to pass as a tepee for the Dakotas who were planning to spend the night.

"How do you people happen to be on this island?" the former con boss bellowed.

His red face was brimming with a fury barely capped by an absurdly cocked derby hat. Attorney Leighton tried the ploy that had worked once, opening his brief case and beginning to read from the treaty: "and the right of such Indian or Indians to enter such tracts of land shall accrue . . ."

"Fight it in court! Don't fight it out here!" Willard cut him off. "You people are trespassing, and I want you off this island before anybody gets scratched. I wouldn't want anybody to get scratched!" With that he shoved one of the photographers aside just to make his own barreling presence more certainly felt. "Get off. Now!"

I have often wondered what Willard really meant by that word, "scratched." He used it several times in the few minutes of that encounter, and I got the impression it must have been something he was used to saying to federal convicts when he meant to warn them that he was going to have their heads beat in or something. In those days, of course, the warning would have been for bad guys trying to escape from Alcatraz, not for Indians trying to set up camp there.

The press and, I must admit, most of us in the general support party, were duly convinced enough by his rage that we began slowly and sheepishly to amble in the general direction of where our hired tugboat still waited at the slip. The Sioux men, nevertheless, held their ground. "This is a peaceful movement," Chalk Cottier tried. "We have a right to claim this property."

"You got no right to trespass here. You're violating the law, and I'm telling you, somebody is going to get scratched up. It better not be any of my people."

"His people" were nowhere in evidence to match our own numbers, but Leighton was becoming more and more convinced about Willard's determination. On the lawyer's advice we packed up the tent and headed for the dock, vowing that the claims had been made and recorded by him anyway, and the courts would have to hear our legitimate case.

Celebrating as we made our way back to Oakland, we passed the boatload of federal marshals headed for the island. The whole thing had lasted about four hours. The next day all the press in the Bay Area carried front page stories about it, relying heavily on clichés about "war parties" and "tom-toms" but fairly and sympathetically stating the case, even under a *San Francisco Examiner* headline that called it a "Wacky Invasion."

The U.S. attorney for that district at the time, a liberal-minded and exceedingly fair black man named Cecil Poole, had been contacted at his own home that Sunday to prepare him for the brewing confrontation.

"They're on the ROCK!?" he replied incredulously to a reporter. "I assume," he went on after a speechless moment, "that they're doing no harm. But Alcatraz is not abandoned. It's being maintained. I'm sympathetic with the Indian question, but even if they really want Alcatraz, it's not mine to give them." Poole neglected to mention that only three days before the Sioux occupation, a specially appointed presidential commission had quietly, if not secretly, met on the island. They had discussed the fact that, despite a full polling, no federal agency could come up with any practical use for the old prison.[4]

Unknowingly Poole had defined the complicated terms of engagement, and opportunity, over an island nobody really seemed to want.

Nobody except, perhaps, Dick McKenzie. Leighton, the lawyer, had meant it when he said that the Sioux intended to press in court their claim to the island. For the next months and years, however, as the sea and the wind and the indecision of the government worked to reclaim the embittered outcropping, the case languished. Even among the Indians it began to lose its symbolic importance when rumors got around that McKenzie was urging the other Dakotas to turn over their individual claims to him.

The last actual court action in the matter was a complaint filed by McKenzie in September of 1965, seeking an injunction against any federal sale of the island or, as an alternative, a directed judgment of $2.5 million to settle his own claim. The case was later dismissed for lack of prosecution.

"No good for nobody," Weatherman, the last Alcatraz convict, had said.

3

The Rock and Hard Places

CERTAINLY, 1964 WASN'T THE FIRST TIME Indians had been on Alcatraz. It wasn't even the first time since Spanish settlers and missionaries had all but obliterated the Coastanoan people native to the region. Indians had been among the first federal prisoners brought to the dungeons on Fort Alcatraz after it was made a federal stockade and prison during the Civil War.

People today, millions of them a year, like to say they've visited Al Capone's cell, or peered in where "the Birdman of Alcatraz," Robert Stroud, thinned away his final years of confinement. They stop and stare, and shudder a bit from the chilly dampness that seems locked into the concrete. But they never see the dungeons deep below the cell block, deeper even than the blank steel cells of solitary. No light reaches down there in the holes cut from solid rock. The darkness is thick and absorbing and seems even to smother the beam of a flashlight for those few who explore the cavernous bowels of the Rock.

Indian prisoners were taken to Alcatraz when the dungeons were still in use. Papagoes, Paiutes, Apaches, Shoshones, Hopis—many who had never before even seen an ocean or felt the sinking cold of blinding fog—were brought in chains on long train rides to Alcatraz for punishment. A few would die there, but many more would be broken in spirit for crimes that in the case of some Hopi prisoners in the 1890s were no greater than refusing to send their children to missionary boarding schools.[1]

Perhaps the most notorious among the Indians sent to Alcatraz were two Modocs from the high pine country of northern California, Slolux and Boncho, who were brought there in 1873.

The trip to the island had begun for them in a way familiar to generations of Native Americans, with an attempt by the Modoc to lay claim to their own land apart from the Klamath reservation further to the north, where the government had ordered them to move. Led by an inspired young Modoc who came to be known as Captain Jack, the tribe left the Klamath and returned to their own hunting grounds, where for a time they lived peacefully with nearby whites. Tensions gradually grew over the exploitation of Indian labor and the retaliation of the Modocs in taking what they felt was owed to them. A military expedition was finally sent to force the Modocs back to Fort Klamath. In two battles, the first a savage barrage on the Modoc camp and the second an ambush led by Captain Jack, both sides suffered many deaths and casualties.

Washington claimed it wanted peace to result from the evident standoff and sent a negotiator known for his sympathies with Indian causes, Maj. Gen. E. R. S. Canby, to talk with Captain Jack. As a translator Canby brought with him a striking young Modoc woman, Wi-ne-ma, who had married a white miner and taken the name Tobey. Tobey was a true heroine of her time, admired by both sides, but there was little she could do to find common ground between Canby's orders to remove the Modoc back to Klamath and Captain Jack's insistence that at a minimum the barren lava beds where the tribe had established its stronghold be made their land.

If Canby sincerely wanted peace, then so did Captain Jack. But Canby was under strict orders, and angry men in Captain Jack's own tribe, including Boncho and Slolux, accused Jack of being an "old woman" by continuing the talks. Even so, Captain Jack tried one more time, and Tobey translated his words to Canby at their next meeting: "Either give us Hat Creek for a home, General, or stop talking."

Canby shook his head "no" for the last time. From a hiding place Slolux and Boncho jumped out, carrying rifles. Captain Jack drew a revolver from his belt and shot Canby in the face.

The series of battles that followed ended in a siege that finally drove the starving Modoc from the lava beds. Captain Jack, betrayed by some of his own people, was captured and hanged. In a gesture of mercy the government sentenced Boncho and Slolux to life on Alcatraz. According to later government figures, the Modoc war cost the United States $450,000, roughly $37,500 for each Modoc killed or executed. The value of the reservation Captain Jack had sought was estimated to be one-twentieth the cost of the war.[2]

Two years after he was imprisoned on Alcatraz, Boncho died the coughing death of consumption. Slolux was released two years after that.

There is much to the story that depicts the agonies of American Indians who in 1964 were thought by most whites to have been sealed and forgotten in history. The surprise to many who read of the Sioux "invasion" that year was learning that there were *any* Indians in the Bay Area, let alone Indians whose native lands were a thousand miles away in the hills and badlands of the Great Plains. Indians by then were curiosities. Souvenirs without current significance.

That is what the government hoped they would remain.

■

Some Americans even today have the sense that reservation life for Native Americans is a good deal. There are no taxes, limited federal regulations, and even immunity from some local laws. They've heard about the poverty, but more recently they've heard about the profits from gambling that make tribes rich. In the 1960s, long before Indian casinos, another common belief among Americans was that most Indians had gotten wealthy from oil wells located on reservation lands. Even Ronald Reagan, who certainly knew better by the time he was president, still fell back on that old political tale about Indians and oil wells when he addressed a group of Russian students in 1988. Perhaps the president was unaware at the time of how the rumored "oil rich" Indians were commonly cheated out of their profits by some of his own bureaucrats.[3]

European Americans have always held such self-contradicting ideas about Indians. "Noble savages" were at once feared for their ferocity and admired for their freedom. Even Custer, in his own writings, longed for the unfettered spirit of the red man.[4] In our own time, Indians are still presented as the models of environmental awareness (even if Hollywood commercial makers are inclined now and then to use Italians who they think "look" more like Indians). Americans are actually proud of Indians, in theory. I can't count how many white folks I've met whose grandmothers were actually "Cherokee princesses." Those Cherokees must have had royalty running all over the place.

Those same "part-Indians," though, seldom know anything about the Trail of Tears along which the government forced the Cherokees on a thousand-mile death march from their native lands in the Carolinas to "Indian Territory" in Oklahoma (where their descendants then supposedly got rich on oil wells). Indians and Indian stories are fine, just so long as they're kept at a distance and told with a generally happy or romantic ending seldom related to the truth.

In the 1960s, far more so than now, few European Americans were consciously aware of any tribal differences among Indians. What they knew was based on the main distinction presented to them by Hollywood—that there were Indians up around Montana somewhere who wore feathers in their hair and were generally known as "Sioux," and other Indians living in the Southwest around Arizona who wore broad headbands and called themselves "Apache." The rest had all been wiped out or sort of just blended in with everybody else. This might sound silly now, but it approximates the hardly realistic view of Indians held by urban Americans in the 1960s.

In part, I think, this view was held because the government wanted it that way. Federal authorities by then were hell-bent on policies that amounted to the "final solution" to the Indian "problem."

By the beginning of that decade federal authorities weren't even sure how many Indians lived in North America. Estimates ranged wildly, anywhere from three hundred to seven hundred thousand. The untallied statistics of the time were evident only to the anthropologists and sociologists, many of whom were studying "dying aboriginal" cultures. Life expectancy for Indians was forty-four years. (At the time the general population's was sixty-five.) Indian infant mortality was twice the national average. Average family income was $1,500 a year, one-fourth the national average. Unemployment among Indians was 40 percent, ten times the national average.[5]

And those were simply the base-line numbers that led to the far more disturbing realities of suicide, alcoholism, and a despairing ignorance of their own cultural traditions. Among the eggheads watching the results, the American Indian seemed all but finished, except in museums and in the movies.

More accurate numbers always existed, however, held in government documents that circulated among bureaucrats and politicians searching for a twentieth-century solution to the "problem" of Indians. During World War II some sixty-five thousand Native Americans left their reservations for service in the military or in war-related industries. The planners of new policies toward Indians took note of the economic results of this population shift and began, during the war, to compile statistics not only on tribal populations but on natural resources contained within tribal lands as well. These studies led to the twin policies of near destruction for the tribes: Termination and Relocation.

In 1952, during yet another of the many historical episodes of social theorizing about the "Indian problem," U.S. Interior Department officials and others prepared an eighteen hundred–page document on tribal populations and organization that knowledgeable Indian scholars recognized as being modeled after the "Doomsday Book" of William the Conqueror. Like that survey of English loyalties in 1085, the Interior Department report to Congress documented conditions of ostensibly sovereign, but captive, states. Indirectly it also drew from the reports compiled during the war to stress the expense and difficulty of maintaining federal trust obligations to sovereign reservations holding the unrealized potential of natural resources on tribal lands. In addition to accounting for timber and water, government statistics estimated that the twenty-three western tribes controlled a third of the nation's low-sulfur coal, fully 80 percent of the country's uranium reserves, and from 3 to 10 percent of national reserves in gas and petroleum. It wasn't enough, for example, that Navajo labor was utilized without taking any precautions at all to mine radioactive minerals on their lands, unaware of their real value or their true hazards. The issue was potential profits as much as it was people.[6]

Treaty obligations to the tribes stood in the way of making full use of these resources. The reports estimated that withdrawing federal services from the reservation system would save millions of dollars every year and allow for the elimination of the decrepit Bureau of Indian Affairs, among the oldest and, by then, the most corrupt bureau in the federal government. Allowing the tribes to become more self-sufficient from the production of their own resources was only a secondary consideration to eliminating the "obstacles" to corporate development.

The "Doomsday Book" of the tribes was drawn from a 1947 report by Assistant BIA Commissioner William T. Zimmerman, Jr., and categorized the tribes most likely to accept "assimilation." The reports became the basis of House Resolution 108 passed by Congress in 1953, and the subsequent Public Law 280 was passed a few days later. Resolution 108 made it a "sense of Congress" that named tribes, including the Oregon Klamaths, the Wisconsin Menominees, and the Chippewas of Turtle Mountain, North Dakota, to be released from federal supervision. The public law followed up that idea by subjecting tribes in California and other states to the criminal and civil laws of their respective states. What scholar and wartime Indian Commissioner John Collier had called the "social genocide" inherent in a policy to integrate Indians into the "mainstream" was now defined in terms of the House resolution: "It is the policy of Congress, as rapidly as possible to make the Indians within the United States subject to the same privileges and responsibilities as are applicable to other citizens of the United States, to end their status as wards of the United States, and to grant them all of the rights and prerogatives pertaining to American citizenship."

In benignly misleading language, the policy of Termination had begun as the final solution to the Indian "problem." Less noticed at the time but soon recognized as Termination's functional twin was the BIA's Relocation Program, expanded beginning in 1952 to include all tribes in a program that was meant to continue the economic lure away from the reservations begun during the war. In 1956 Public Law 959 made Relocation part of official policy, intending forever to change the Indian way of life.[7]

Follow me on our journey that made some of us part of this story even before we knew it.

■

La Nada Boyer was five or six years old when Termination became policy in Washington. She was one of twelve children in her family living on the Shoshone-Bannock reservation at Fort Hall, Idaho, near Pocatello.

Fort Hall can be a bleak and discouraging place on the wind-lashed plains of southern Idaho. Many of the people raise cattle and struggle with the dry land agriculture that is the basis of the tribe's economy. When La Nada was a child the poverty and the racism among nearby whites were bitterly apparent even to hungry young Indian kids like her. In the nearby town of Blackfoot there were signs in shop windows that said, "No Indians or Dogs Allowed."[8]

How could a little girl barely able to make sense of such words understand that in 1953 the government was determined to end her "status" as a "ward" of the United States and grant her "prerogatives" she didn't know were missing?

The government itself seemed perplexed at the problem it had created. If it was going to "terminate" the reservations, what was it going to do with the Indians who lived on them? Generations of neglect and abuse of what little education system existed on the reservations only compounded the problem of people having few skills or experience beyond what they had learned in a struggle to survive in the most isolated and poorest regions of America.

For nearly a century the government's answer had been to wrench away children from their own families, and send them off to distant boarding schools fashioned in missionary style under the leadership of religiously oriented government employees whose task it was to remove the "Indianness" from the children by cutting their hair, denying them the use of their own languages, and, when they thought it appropriate, beating the devil out of them.

I spent ten years of my life in such a school at Pipestone, Minnesota, from 1935 to 1945. Although I endured the scarring heartache of being taken from my own family when I was five and being trained in regimented order to grasp and celebrate what seemed like cultural absurdities of "Pilgrim" Thanksgivings and "Amens" to blessings I couldn't understand before breakfast, let alone dinner, I still had it better than many other Indian children who suffered more.

Graduation at Pipestone Indian Training School, May 1945. Adam (Nordwall) Fortunate Eagle in center. Photograph courtesy of author.

We at least knew we were "Indian" at Pipestone, even if we could not speak in our own languages or be taught anything about the ways of our own people. Because the school had federal funding, at least we were not forced, as other Indian kids in missionary schools had been, to see our families as sinful "pagans." Instead we were taught to believe there was a "better way."

There has always been, in my memory at least, that portion of federal "wisdom" which suggested that somehow if young Indians could be shown how much better it was to at least "act white," they would gradually blend in and be embraced among all the understanding grandchildren of "Cherokee princesses."

My own experience took me from Pipestone to Haskell Institute in Kansas, a sort of high school and junior college for Indians at the time, where I was taught a trade and was able to perfect some of my own natural talents and inclination for art. It was by chance, really, that I wound up in San Francisco where my mother had moved and where I waited for a call that never came from the military during the Korean War.

I met my wife, Bobbie, at Haskell. She was studying secretarial arts, and I was already what they called an "old head" at the school, encouraged by my instructors to develop doodling talents I had learned at Pipestone into a career in commercial art. By that they meant painting billboards, not cre-

Bobbie Graham and Adam Nordwall as students at Haskell Institute. Photograph courtesy of Bobbie Graham.

ating new images. Though it had nothing to do with the nickname by which she is known even to our children, Bobbie was truly one of the most stunning "bobby-soxers" of the time. As a couple in the old photos we look much like any pair of teenagers in America who found their idol in Frank Sinatra. I was a little astonished when she told me her father raised turkeys, not cattle or horses, in Nevada, but she found some surprise in my long years of making a family out of boarding school, too. We were married in 1949, but for the first six months of our marriage we were separated while Bobbie worked as a secretary for the Stewart Indian School in Nevada and I finished my graduate studies in commercial art at Haskell.

That winter, I got my first job—drawing magazine advertisements and layouts for Centaur Studios in Kansas City—and Bobbie and I were reunited. Had it not been for the Korean War, Kansas City is where we might have stayed. All four of my brothers were called up to serve in the war. I was the youngest and last of my mother's sons, and she expected that I would be next to go. She was living in San Francisco then, and wanted the two of us to spend time with her before I was called into service. Bobbie was pregnant with our first child, Cheri, when we took the $300 we had in savings and packed everything we owned into three suitcases for the move to San Francisco. My mother had found a temporary job for me at a termite extermination company. We rented a tiny apartment and set up housekeeping on the $48 a week I earned after taxes.

We all thought this would be a temporary situation, but I guess in part because I had a job and a young family, the call to the military never came. A year later, at the age of twenty-one, I passed the state exam to become a licensed termite inspector and began a career that would lead to a business of my own.

"Termination," beyond what it implied in my business, meant little to me in 1953. I had endured the mindless wit of coworkers and clients who called me "Chief," and the stupid gestures some of them made with their fingers, pretending to show feathers while they grinned and mocked a "war dance." Meeting a "real Indian" was an unusual experience for them. I knew that, and I knew that my bearing their ignorant insults with good humor in its own way helped my business. At that time it was not big news in the cities that the federal government had decided to end the "problem" of the reservations.

Yet federal authorities themselves were not so ignorant as to think they could simply conclude two hundred years of agreements with sovereign peoples by declaring them to be "assimilated." Something else had to be done to take the "Indian-ness" out of Indians.

The government's answer was that other program intended to reduce the reservation population by offering technical training and job opportunities to Indians, younger ones especially, who were willing to leave the agrarian reservations and enter what federal analysts now envisioned as "urbanized" America. Relocation was sold to the tribes in the same way the Termination policy had been, with great promises of new opportunities in job training and guaranteed employment; it promised a whole new way of life outside the poverty of the reservation.

By 1958 eight cities were designated as sites for new Relocation centers. Three of them were in California: in Los Angeles, San Jose, and Oakland. They offered training and employment assistance in everything from auto mechanics to the newly emerging field of electronics, provided that Indians accepting the offer fulfilled their obligation to federal policy during the

Young Indians being trained at Pacific Automotive Center, a car mechanics schools in Oakland, California. Photograph by Ilka Hartmann.

months (and sometimes a year or more) before they became independent in their new place in urban America.

It was a voluntary program cast into the reservations like bait on a long line. Unemployed men and women, and even whole families, were offered the opportunity by the BIA to sign up for training and employment in a "meaningful job" somewhere else. Usually it was hundreds of miles from their reservation homes, and never was it on or near the reservation itself.

Still, a lot of Indians, young people especially, elected to take the chance. They were given one-way bus tickets to whichever city they chose, and told to report to the Relocation office where housing would be provided for them and a program begun to get them on their way to personal success. Characteristically, the housing was a small apartment somewhere in a ghetto nearly as poor as the reservation had been. Every day the relocatee was told to report to the office and wait, often staring at the flickering numbness of a TV set, while an "employment assistance officer" worked to set up a job interview. Families left waiting at their new homes seldom ventured out into fearsome neighborhoods so unlike where they had come from. If the Indian relocatee did not show up at the office every day, subsistence for the entire family was cut off.

Indian family in San Francisco. Photograph by Ilka Hartmann.

Work would, eventually, be found for the relocatee, and government assistance would end after the first paycheck. Many of the jobs proved to be temporary, however, and when they ended the Indian family members found themselves stranded, castaways in a strange and often hostile environment.

La Nada by then had been sent from Fort Hall to the St. Mary's School for Indian Girls in Springfield, South Dakota, where the young women were given special training in laundry work and housekeeping. She was expelled at age thirteen for being "too outspoken."[9]

By then the federal policies that would soon converge all our fates were in full operation. Termination had taken hold and been put in effect, especially on the smaller reservations and "rancherias" of the West Coast where little trouble or organized opposition could be expected from tribal members suddenly awarded the "full privileges" of U.S. citizenship (including the right to sell their land to eagerly waiting entrepreneurs, both Indian and white). One small irony is that one of the first reservations thus terminated

The Nordwall family in San Leandro, circa 1961. *Left to right*: Julie, Adam, Adam Sr., Cheri, and Bobbie. Photograph courtesy of author.

was at Fort Klamath, where Captain Jack and the Modocs had begun their resistance.

Bobbie and I had enlarged our family with another daughter and a son, and I was successful enough to open my own business, The First American Termite Company of San Leandro. We bought a comfortable home near the suburban school there and began a family routine that fit all the postwar consumer models. Without any government help we were beginning to live the "good life" of the American middle class.

As a little boy at Pipestone School I had often felt embarrassed by the Swedish heritage brought by my father to my Chippewa family. It left me with a short pug nose not anywhere near as handsome as the prominent features of my Sioux and Cheyenne friends at the school. Secretly, when I was just a boy of seven or eight, I used to stand in front of the mirror in the washroom and pull and pull on my nose, hoping to make it bigger. In San Leandro, however, I had to admit that "assimilation" had its advantages. If I wanted to, I could pass as white.

Bobbie and I took our three children on trips either to my reservation at Red Lake, Minnesota, or to Bobbie's Shoshone-Paiute home outside Fallon, Nevada. But those early days were like tourist excursions for us back to places we could only visit and introduce to the children. We had no thought then of staying long. Our future, clearly, was invested in another world.

■

Twice more, once at the Chilocco Indian Boarding School in Oklahoma and later at Stewart Indian School in Carson City, Nevada, La Nada found herself labeled "difficult" and given a bus ticket back to Fort Hall. She managed a semester at Idaho State College before dropping out and finding herself adrift again at the age of seventeen. This time she asked the BIA for Relocation, and accepted the bus ticket they gave her to the San Francisco Bay Area. At Fort Hall nearly 80 percent of the Indians who had accepted Relocation had returned to the reservation within a year. The few who had successfully left referred to the others as "going back to the blanket."

For us, the difference between what we were becoming as a successful suburban family with bowling league credentials and what was then thought of as "blanket" Indians still locked in the past was made not more apparent, but increasingly more meaningful.

If the BIA had hoped that Relocation would make Indians vanish into the mainstream of society, they miscalculated. The loneliness and isolation that was so much a part of the Relocation Program proved to be its only point of redemption. Indian people cut off from their own families and their own tribal cultures sought out each other in a kinship among tribes that many of them had never known before. Sioux and Navajo. Chippewa and Apache. Mohawk and Shoshone. It was like a convergence of captive nations, as unlike each other in some ways as the British and French, but as much alike in others as the Irish on St. Patrick's Day.

For us the gatherings first began at Sunday picnics at an Oakland or East Bay park, where an effort would be made to welcome newcomers and help them feel a little more comfortable with their surroundings. There was a sense of reunion to it, as when I occasionally met young men I had known at Pipestone when they passed through the Bay Area on their way to or from the war. It was at those picnics, which soon added a drum or some simple social dancing on a park-groomed lawn, where the rhythm of a seriously pan-tribal movement first began to be heard. We felt a sense of renewed pride from these gatherings, something old and yet uniquely new. Something we wanted to be part of.

I remember my earliest attempts at preparing for one of these events when I outfitted our small son, Addie, in the head of a fox fur stole I found at a Goodwill store and myself in a turkey feather contraption I thought from childhood memory approximated something Chippewa. I included around my ankles little "tinkle, tinkle, tinkle" Christmas bells about one-third the size of those worn by the real traditional dancers I was pretending to be. At that weekend's picnic and powwow these outfittings felt like a way of coming home at last.

Someone pointed out a stony-faced fellow staring at me with his arms folded across his chest. "I think he's from your tribe," they said, in what I took to be almost a warning. Critical as he could sometimes be, Cy Williams and I would become lifelong friends from that day until his death a few years ago. Cy and his wife, Aggie, were from the Cass Lake Chippewa Reservation in Minnesota, just fifty miles from my own home. Without really intending to, Cy had become something of a success story for the Relocation Program, working as a machinist in Oakland. He was successful enough at this job that he had no intention of giving it up to return to the reservation, but that didn't mean he had forgotten his roots.

Cy was a gritty, tough-talking, blue-collar kind of guy, who also collected trinkets. The trinkets were all he could find to remind him, and anyone who came near him, of his own "Indian-ness." They were silly little things, some of them, just plastic toy figures of little red warriors or glazed salt shakers with apparently Indian designs. Cy and Aggie's pin-neat cottage in Oakland was full of the trinkets, carefully dusted and kept in place. On Cy's old blue panel van were plastered bumper strips advertising road-stop curio shops and tourist attractions with Indian themes, and on the dashboard he had little dolls clad in buckskin, and beaded necklaces like Boy Scouts make, and decals from schools with Indian mascots. Cy understood their triviality and had much deeper knowledge from his own experience about true tribal tradition. But in Oakland, in those days, the trinkets and the decals were all that Cy could find around him to express who he was. He had a word for those things he collected and kept, a word all his own that he applied to whatever he thought qualified. If it was close, if it reminded him enough of home, Cy called it "Indi-onish."

Bit by bit, with Cy's help and instruction, I began to replace my old Christmas-bell costume with a more authentic outfit and a more meaningful outlook. The picnics grew into regular powwows. The gatherings created new gatherings of the Navajo Club or the Sioux Club or the Four Winds Club. All were results the federal planners of Relocation had not anticipated.

But for the younger people, those who had been detached from their reservations and their families in the same period that federal policy stressed Termination, the road "home" was even more complicated. La Nada's problems with Relocation were not untypical. She waited like the others in

Calumet Dance at Yoeul Field, Oakland, California, ca. 1964. *Left to right*: Jack Orr (Shoshone), Cy William (Chippewa), unknown dancer, Adam Fortunate Eagle (Chippewa). Photograph courtesy of author.

the Oakland office, daily expecting something. When something came it was a series of temporary clerking jobs that she had found herself. Cut off from BIA support, she took yet another route followed by some of the relocatees and began working as a barmaid in one of the beer parlors of what was becoming an Indianized "ghetto" in a corner of San Francisco's Mission District. She was young, bright, and pretty, and she was living in a city that had always favored youth and beauty. For her and other young people our powwows and picnics were no more than another dead-end trip to the "blanket." Before she was eighteen she was pregnant and alone in the city.

We didn't know each other then. Even Indians had no real sense among themselves of how what we had in common also kept us apart. It came as a surprise to most people in the Bay Area when the press reported in 1964 that Sioux Indians had occupied Alcatraz. Until then most of that urban population had no idea there were Indians living around the Bay. They were, after all, invisible.

4

"Indi-onish" America

CY USED TO THROW HIS ARMS across his chest in a sudden gesture and huff out his disgust. "Ah, the hell with it," he'd say. "The hell with it." In our backyard, as he taught me and six-year-old Addie what he knew of traditional dancing and Chippewa styles, we talked often about the frustration he felt with the federal Relocation Program and "white people" in general. The program had worked for him and Aggie, at least in so far as it had given him the opportunity for a job where his own skills could bring him greater and greater financial success as a machinist. But Cy saw how Relocation had failed so many younger Indians, leaving them helpless in the city and begging rides into more uncertain despair "back home" on their reservations. His frustration would build with the attempts he made to explain it to the BIA officials who merely shook their heads and repeated back their rules to him.

"Ah, the hell with it," he'd say all at once. "The hell with it." But he never meant that.

Like the trinkets with which he decorated his life, Cy tried to involve himself in every "Indi-onish" activity he could find that would help tribal people. He joined every club he could and signed up in support of any cause remotely on behalf of Indians. By 1961 he had become an active member of the board of directors of the American Friends Service Committee, or Quaker, group that was then establishing what they called the Intertribal Friendship House in Oakland.

"These guys on the board are mostly white people," he told me. "A bunch of good-hearted Quakers who still don't know much about Indians. We should be doing that. They don't know. They should be helping *us* run programs for Indians, not getting us to help them!"

That was Cy. He really respected the Friends on the board with him and

Bowling friends, 1960s. Photograph courtesy of author.

appreciated what they were trying to do, but most of all he wanted Indians in charge. He wanted an Indian with more experience than himself in business matters and in general protocol to take charge somehow of those well-meaning white people before they did more damage. He nominated me.

Without Cy's influence I suppose my own life might have taken an entirely different direction. What the government unintentionally presented in cities like San Francisco and Oakland at that time was an opportunity for Indians who were not only uncertain about their futures, but, thanks to almost a century of demeaning and banning their customs and of blocking the education of their children, were also by then uncertain about their pasts. They started meeting each other in places strange to all of them and, ironically, it was in those places they began to rediscover their own identities.

Bobbie and I and the kids went to the picnics at Golden Gate Park and, later, at Knowland Park in Oakland; we watched as the social gatherings on a Sunday began to evolve into a pan-tribal powwow through which our

The Navajo Club at Yoeul Field, Oakland, California, circa 1965. Photograph courtesy of author.

commonalities were often expressed in the richly colorful cultural distinctions between us. I and my family were mostly observers at first, there only for the socializing, the gossipy reunion. We had no serious thoughts, as others had, of giving up and going "home" to the reservation.

Our own social set, which Cy and Aggie became part of, revolved in large part around the three bowling leagues in which we participated. My greatest achievement at the time was the "King of the Lanes" trophy I had won at Manor Bowl near our home. I was a success at who I was becoming, and it was only gradually during those weekend afternoons among the steadily growing numbers of Indian people relocated from their homes that I began to find a new focus in my life.

"Well, damn it, somebody needs to get this together," Cy said. "You need to get involved, Nordwall."

I don't think I was reluctant or unwilling, or even coy about taking on the job. That didn't sound like me, and besides, at the time I felt a confidence, almost like making a new discovery.

One by one I began contacting the leaders of all the tribal clubs that had been formed since the picnics began—the Navajo Club, the Four Winds, the Sports Club. The problem Cy realized (and that many of the others could see coming) was the Sioux Club, and its dominance of the picnic and pow-wow organization. The club was headed by Richard McKenzie, a powerful figure who seemed to stress his own tribal, and even ethnic, superiority.

We organized a mass meeting at the newly opened Friendship House where for the first time the leaders of the other clubs began openly talking about making the picnic and powwow organization more democratic. It was an awkward time for Dick McKenzie. Since the weekend events had moved to Knowland Park, we had begun to charge an admission fee and a fee for booths, money that would be used to pay the costs for the next event. Dick had found himself in charge before there was really an organization. Now doubts were surfacing about his style of dominant leadership.

Although we worked together for many years to come, including during the 1964 episode at Alcatraz, I don't think Dick ever forgave me for organizing that meeting at which I was elected president of the picnic and pow-wow committee. There was $200 in the fund, which Dick turned over. The next year I was able to turn over $1000 to the committee before I resigned as president.

The little rebellion against Sioux dominance was perhaps most indicative of how quickly an urban Indian community was developing in the early sixties. The needs of that community for basic assistance and help in coping with city life soon outgrew the social satisfaction from picnics and pow-wows alone. With the assistance of the American Friends Service Committee we formed the United Bay Area Council of American Indians, and set a charter for ourselves almost as a new and unique tribe the government had never anticipated. I was elected chairman of the council in 1962.

We met at the Friendship House every Wednesday night at 7:30, or as near to that hour as the invariably late "Indian time" would allow. We'd arrange the banquet tables in a large open-center square with plenty of room for the representatives of every club and group associated with the council. You need to know how tricky that could be. This wasn't just a gathering like the United Nations. Sometimes it was more like asking the lions to talk it over with the lambs. Some tribal differences ran deep and arose from centuries of dispute. Some tribes were almost unknown to each other, as if being a Haida-Tlingit was like being an alien from another planet to a Navajo or a Cheyenne. Just being "Indian" wasn't always enough to assure a fraternal feeling.[1]

Once again it was the actions of the government trying to eliminate us that served most to bring us together. No matter what long-standing differences the Hopi might have had with the Navajo, everyone could understand Horace Spencer's story of being brought by the BIA from Shiprock and then abandoned in Oakland with his wife and eight children. They could feel the

INTERTRIBAL FRIENDSHIP HOUSE
OPEN WED. thru SUN. 2 to 10:30 P.M.

Sarah Brown (Pomo) with her niece Tina and nephew Anthony Fourkiller at the Intertribal Friendship House in Oakland, California. Photograph by Ilka Hartmann.

quiet spoken confusion of Jim and Alvina Brown telling how their Pomo reservation at Clear Lake was abruptly terminated.[2]

What really went around those tables was an exchange of news among the people, as the information spread one to another about what was being planned for us all. We did what we could to help individual families, but we operated without any funding except what we were able to earn from one big annual Memorial Day weekend powwow and "show" that we advertised to white audiences.

One of the first Memorial Day events was held at Bret Harte School in Hayward, which boasted a grand amphitheater around the field, perfect for our needs. At first, though, the school district officials couldn't understand when I told them we would need some room for camping. It was part of the

Grand entry at Yoeul Field, Oakland, California, 1964.
Left to right: Bobbie Nordwall (Shoshone), Belva Cottier (Sioux), Adam Fortunate Eagle (Chippewa), Al "Chalk" Cottier (Sioux). Photograph courtesy of author.

cultural sense of it, I explained, being close to the earth for those two days. Reluctantly they gave us space on the lawn in front of the school, and I was delighted to see the array of tepees and small tents that sprang up there on Friday evening.

Strolling past the little children darting about and women clinking pans or rolling out blankets, I noticed Jones Benally, a lanky young Navajo hoop dancer, who seemed transfixed in a leg-folded posture and staring intently at the ground. I was concerned that something might be wrong, and I stopped and stared until Jones glanced up at me and shot me a big, shy grin.

"Making medicine," he said. "Woman medicine." He winked, and went back to whatever he was seeing in the ground.

The powwow performance was a great success. One advantage we had in those days was that suburban families were always drawn to the events. They had a lot of curiosity about Indians in the "old way," even if they did step cautiously around some of our own less savory characters whom we diligently tried to keep from weaving into booth and food areas. We sold no beer or alcohol and strictly banned it from the grounds, but, as I was to learn again and again, booze is a powerful force to contend with in Indian affairs.

All in all, though, I was proud of how it had gone. Sometime after mid-

Pat Jackson, Bay Area
Princess of 1971. Mrs.
Jackson, of the
Chippewa Club, was a
member of the
Intertribal Dancers and
the United Council.
Oakland Museum
Memorial Day Pow
Wow, 1971.
Photograph by Ilka
Hartmann.

night I strolled back through our camp area on the front lawn and noticed
Jones again, this time intensely engaged in an embrace with a young lady.
Worked for him, I guess.

It was about 2:00 A.M. that I started hearing the first shrieks and howls.
Immediately I imagined one of the drunks had come back and begun big
trouble. And yet, as my head cleared, it didn't sound like a fight or an ar-
gument. There was laughter in the yelling. Whoops among the squeals.

"It's raining in my tent!" I heard. "It's raining UP!"

Men, women, and children were stumbling around in chaos, scooping up
bundles of soaked clothing, laughing and cursing all at once. Bret Harte
School, it turned out, was one of the early innovators in switching from the
old hose methods to underground sprinklers. Perhaps the school district
official who let us use the grounds did not himself know that they operated
on a timer.

Things like that—the unexpected shared things—have a way of binding people together in good humor for a long time afterward. We always cherished those good times and remember them more, I suppose, than some of the worst times.

They say that every American alive at the time can remember precisely what they were doing when they heard the news that Kennedy had been shot. I was at the termite company working over the books with Bobbie. Among Indians the news spread with shock and grief, the same way it did everywhere else that November of 1963. As a people, as an American "minority," I cannot say, however, that we felt any particular loss. The great promise that Kennedy and his New Frontier seemed to offer others did not come to us in any way that we could see would make a difference. Termination and Relocation policies begun in the Eisenhower administration went on. Even if a Democratic administration was perhaps more culturally enlightened, the bureaucracy of the BIA proceeded in its usual way. On the reservations, that acronym stood for "Boss Indians Around," and it meant clearly that no matter which tribal government might exist in name, the federal agency was in charge of everything—from bare necessities to the tools needed to tend a garden of one's own.

Despite the obvious failures of Relocation that saw many people return to the reservation and many others fall into slums of despair and alcohol in the cities, federal statistics estimated that by 1967 more than 61,000 Indians had been given Relocation "assistance" away from their reservation homes, nearly as many as had left during the war. But those numbers didn't tell the whole story. The BIA itself estimated that, when combined with Adult Vocational Education programs and the effects of Termination, "approximately 200,000 Indians [had] been moved to urban areas in the last ten years" [between 1958 and 1968].[3] There had not been such mass removal of Native Americans since the Trail of Tears in 1838 that had forced the Cherokee into Oklahoma Territory.

Actual termination of the tribes, although slower under Democratic administrations, still continued, especially on the West Coast and in the old Indian territories of the Midwest. By 1969, according to recent research, 109 Indian reservations, rancherias, and bands of Indians had been officially "terminated" out of existence.[4]

The strongest hope we had to cling to was no longer in the BIA-dependent tribal organizations themselves that struggled, reservation by reservation, to contend with the relentless poverty and rural racism. The focus on the future of American Indians was in breaking away from agency control and turning more and more toward the pan-Indian movement forced into creation by the actions of the government itself.

In the Midwest (which to us seemed like the East), where more young Indians had successfully found their way into higher education, the beginnings of protest were formed in Chicago around the National Indian Youth Council (NIYC) and its keenly intelligent student leaders such as Mel Thom and Clyde Warrior. NIYC had an impact on its times and claimed within two or three short years to have doubled and then tripled its membership.[5] That might have been a growth of only six to eighteen, but the point was made. Indians all over the country were taking on a different presence than they had ever before held in North America. What had been sovereign nations that dealt directly with Washington by means of war or treaty, now had to become part of a cultural and racial force in the society—a movement that could not be minimized or divided. In 1888 a Nevada Paiute named Wovoka had a vision about all Indian people coming together, restoring the buffalo and bringing the dead back to life. The idea of Wovoka's Ghost Dance frightened white people and led to the 1890 massacre of Big Foot and his people at Wounded Knee.

What was happening in the 1960s was not the start of another Ghost Dance but a transition from the time when we could no longer survive separate and apart from our mutual interests. Indians would never regard themselves as minorities in their own land and they resented being associated with the racial aims of blacks and others. It was hard for many of them to accept, but it could not be denied, that if any group had reason to demand respect for their civil rights by the U.S. government, it was the Indians. Yet even the 1964 Civil Rights Act had specifically excluded Indians as deserving of equal justice.

All around us, and in the Bay Area especially, a social storm was rising over equal rights for those they called "Negroes" then, and over demands by college students at Berkeley for more autonomy in their own affairs. We watched from a quiet distance, aware of their frustrations but separated from their aims. In one way, I suppose, we still felt we had much more to lose than did they by campaigning for mere social recognition. It was our land that was being taken, our culture. We didn't want just an equal place in society. We wanted what was ours alone.

In Denver, Vine Deloria, Jr., a Standing Rock Sioux who was working with the White Buffalo Council and the United Scholarship Service, had begun what would become a lifetime of scholarly research and stinging analysis with what seemed to many at first like a joke. "Custer died for your sins" was Vine's coinage. Long before it became a book title, Vine distributed it as a bumper strip. White people in general were accustomed to thinking that somber, silent Indians had no sense of humor at all. They were trained by their own movie culture to think of it as the "Custer massacre" in which the brave Yellow Hair held out to the very end. But they got Vine's joke immediately, and something deeper in their consciences made them admit it wasn't so funny after all. Vine would follow it up with slogans like, "Custer wore an arrow shirt." Clever, meaningful messages that perhaps amounted to the first Indian public relations campaign in history.

Buffy Sainte Marie, a Cree from Canada, found her way into the more eclectic college consciousness of the time with folk songs that were bitter poems on the abuses of the nineteenth century. In her songs she told the stories of small pox–infested blankets that wiped out whole bands, of lies and treachery that only some of us had heard from our own elders. Among us younger intellectuals especially, she gained ground, and heart, that we had not found before.

But if Indians were finding their own place in the minds of white liberals as part of the fashionably guilty awareness of historical abuses, the situation was short of giving most Americans a grasp of the agony that still went on in the official movement to eliminate Indians as more than noble losers.

Lyndon Johnson at least said more about it than Kennedy had. The new president promised to put in place a "War on Poverty" in America that would address the Great Society's greatest contradictions. He was certainly inspired more by Edward R. Murrow's view of migrant labor in the CBS film documentary "Harvest of Shame" than by the even more stark evidence of destitution and bigotry visible on the reservations that could have been, but never was, presented by his own Bureau of Indian Affairs. Nevertheless, Indians and the reservation system had a part in what Johnson's sociologist advisors recognized must be taken seriously if a war on poverty were to amount to more than rhetoric.

In May 1964, two months after our first mission to Alcatraz, I was invited as chairman of the United Bay Area Council to attend the first Capitol Conference on Poverty to be held in Washington D.C. That's where the one suit that I have comes from. I bought it from a tailor at the insistence of Jack LaRue of the Oakland Radio Electronics Training School (RETS)— a Relocation facility in Oakland. Jack was the classic "pinky ring and bombast" white business hustler of his time, and I'm sure he sensed an opportunity for himself in the federally funded programs Johnson was proposing. But, however much we knew he might want to exploit that easy government money, we couldn't deny that Jack and RETS had been helpful to the United Council in providing job training and some career opportunities to young Indians. LaRue regarded me as something of a protégé in such business and insisted I should carry that tailored image to Washington. At least I wore a beaded bolo instead of a knotted tie when I got there.

If I'm making Jack out to be an overstaged image of his time, I suppose

Adam Fortunate Eagle (right) and fellow delegate at the Capitol Conference on Poverty, Washington, D.C., 1964. Photograph by Bettye Lane. Photograph courtesy of author.

in many ways I, too, was seen with some of the same suspicion by other Indians. My business was going well. Bobbie and I drove a new Cadillac, perhaps less aware of its symbolism than we realized. But I believed that success spoke of confidence and, if anything, my desire to show it made me even more dedicated to spending an increasingly large amount of time to the United Council.

Chalk Cottier, representing the Sioux Club, and I went to the D.C. conference. Philleo Nash, Lyndon Johnson's gregarious commissioner of the BIA, was there to greet us, along with an assortment of senators and congressmen, all repeating the line that the president intended to put Indians first in defeating poverty.

Being business ready, I certainly believed my skills were enough to enmesh myself in the series of workshops the conference proposed. I was even elected chairman of the Economic Development Committee, whose task was to establish a plan for new opportunities on or near the reservations. My committee worked on its report until 2:00 A.M., and the next day at the general session the conference assembly praised it as containing the conference's most practical suggestions. That was not the only time I'd hear such encouraging words. It was, however, the last time that I was quite so innocently enthusiastic to believe them.

Again and again the federal government collided with its own contradictions on Indian policy. If the Office of Economic Opportunity (OEO) was serious about attacking poverty on the reservations, how did that conform with the enforced poverty still being brought about by BIA Relocation and its attempt to "assimilate" Indians in time to "terminate" their tribal rights? Tribal councils knew better than to trust one federal agency working against another. They accepted what help they could get, but still let it be known that a better answer, and the only legitimate answer, was to stop interference in development of what was rightfully the councils' alone.

It was during this time, while I was still devoted to the hopeful promises of Johnson's OEO, that I first met Tim Findley, on terms that once again led this journey on the turtle's back in a fateful circle. Findley, a former marine and before that a civil rights "freedom rider," found himself as a very young man spearheading a program for the War on Poverty's domestic Peace Corps, or VISTA. The intention was to recruit more young Indians themselves as VISTA volunteers who could be trained and sent to their own or other reservations with skills to develop self-help programs. In theory the so-called Project America effort had some promise, but Findley was meeting with great reluctance and distrust among the young Indians themselves, especially among the rising militants of the National Indian Youth Council, for example, to whom another government program was seen as just another sham.

In part to aid with the effort, the OEO had produced a promotional film that showed (for perhaps the first time) some of the true conditions on the reservations that existed under government sponsorship. Findley had obtained the first print of that film, and was bringing it with him in a scheduled visit to the United Council where he hoped to review it before several young Indians involved in Relocation. But he had moved too quickly. Even as he was flying to San Francisco a new decision had been made in Washington to withdraw the film. Something of what it said about reservation life did not conform with federal policy.

Findley called us from his hotel, concerned that he had arrived to find a message already waiting for him that meant he would have to cancel the promised showing. To Tim it was a double-cross. He was changing hotels and intended to show the film anyway, he said.

We met him the next evening at a Chinatown restaurant and bar he suggested. He was scheduled to show the film the following morning. Just how a young senior bureaucrat from Washington found us in that restaurant, none of us may ever know. Findley was first shocked and then increasingly furious when the dapper government man strolled up to the bar, demanding by his presence to be introduced to Bobbie and me. The two of us could see that this was not going to go well. At the first opportunity both Bobbie and I excused ourselves for a moment.

When we returned, the young senior bureaucrat was picking himself up off the floor and the excited Chinese bartender was urging Tim to leave immediately. We never saw the film, and it would be a couple of years before we saw Findley again.

5

Scalping Columbus

ONLY TWO MONTHS AFTER that first Capitol Conference on Poverty, those of us designated by various organizations convened again in Fresno, this time concentrating on the California reservations and rancherias in particular as the very sort of "fronts" that BIA Commissioner Philleo Nash and, indirectly, President Johnson himself had identified in the "war" to end the unequal distribution of wealth in America.

That, at least, is what we thought it meant, and from what we had been told in Washington we had every reason to believe that proposals made in our Economic Development Committee for funded and supported efforts to establish new initiatives in or around the reservations themselves would be a part of the appropriations bill for the new Office of Economic Opportunity.

As I traveled to Fresno I also carried with me that more intangible sense of enthusiasm that still came from the occupation incident on Alcatraz. It was theater, sure, a headline and a few striking photos in black and white. It might have been called "wacky," but within two days news of it had spread all around the world. Nothing else in all the contemporary, and often depressing, reality about American Indians and their rights had claimed nearly as much attention in the previous seventy years. There was a sense that something was bound to happen. Some change was coming on the political winds, so long as we could press on with the momentum.

From the Fresno conference emerged not only more of the same kind of confidence, but the beginning of the Inter Tribal Council (ITC) of California, for the first time linking all the tribes of the politically potent Golden State in one association. Al Elgin, a Pomo, became its first president. In part because of my success in drawing together the economic development proposals made in Washington, I was given the nonpaying job of interim executive director. This was a great honor for me as someone from a tribe out-side California. It was also a sign of how serious and business-like the ITC intended to be about staking its claims in the promised new federal policies.

How positive it all seemed. And yet, perhaps we devoted too little attention to what still stood in our way.

In June of 1953, two months before Congress passed its Termination Act, the California State Assembly sent a memorandum to Congress and the president saying the Bureau of Indian Affairs "has outlived its usefulness" and assuring Washington that California "is able to provide for the well-being of American Indians, as it does for other citizens, by laws of general applicability." Without bothering with the sort of flowery promises about "rights and prerogatives" that dressed up the federal act, California's position was made bluntly clear: "The Legislature of the State of California respectfully memorializes the President and Congress of the United States to take such steps as are necessary to effect a termination of the authority of the Bureau of Indian Affairs, particularly in the State of California."[1]

Ten years later, as federal authorities proceeded with the policy to put California tribes under "general applicability" through Termination, we found ourselves meeting with a different set of federal and state bureaucrats specifically concerned with directing poverty money to the remaining reservations and rancherias. The contradiction was apparent to none of us. Yet.

That was also the year my bowling career ended. First at Cy's urgings, and then with the support of the United Council in electing me as co-chairman (along with Al Hicks, a Navajo), and finally my own growing enthusiasm for what seemed to be a new awakening in Washington, absorbed almost all my time.

I won't say the termite business suffered. Both Bobbie and I still worked hard on its demanding daily details. But it was a time when perhaps the business might have grown more and I might have been seen with a different regard among the industry than what would be the eventual result. I had made my own decision about assimilation and I would never come that close to it again.

Among American Indians of many tribes and cultural traditions there had evolved social categories similar, and yet uniquely distinct, in the patterns set by the "melting pot" of the United States. There were reservation Indians and urban Indians; traditional Indians and powwow Indians; Indians who knew their own tribal language and customs, and Indians who knew virtually nothing at all about their own tribes. These were conditions in many ways created and enforced by two centuries of federal actions both cruel and well-meaning. The combination of Termination and Relocation in the 1950s and 1960s had drawn these differences into even sharper contrast.

We did not find it to be a simple matter of moving from the social and mutually supportive gatherings of weekend picnics (or even the spontane-ous development of dancing and singing together) into what has been imag-ined by others as a unified political or racial movement. Far to the contrary, there were many contradictions and conflicts among us, some of them tribal, some of them personal. Many of us, drawn to different spheres or having other ambitions, did not even know each other, and did not care to.

Yet there was always someone trying to represent the American Indian, trying to cast the image of the Indian in the great "pageant" of America. We had all seen the movies since when we were children, and had even caught ourselves now and then cheering for the wrong side. Games of cowboy and Indian were made from a history of genocide, as if in the next century chil-dren might play Nazi and Jew. But we never saw it that way. We could be offended, but just as often we were amused at how we were portrayed.

It was with that in mind that Cy first started urging, and finally demand-ing, that we watch the Italians doing their annual re-enactment of Colum-bus discovering the New World at the San Francisco Marina.

"They got Boy Scouts doing Indians!" Cy said, almost wheezing with indignation. Not that Boy Scouts (in this case actually Sea Scouts) doing Indians was anything particularly new, but to Cy it was just too close to home to go unexamined.

Including all our kids there were about fifteen of us from four families who at last agreed to make a picnic and outing of it by spreading our blan-kets on the marina lawn, just a little apart from the throngs of people cov-ering the bleachers and the grassy hillside along the small yacht harbor.

True to the event's publicity, the "Indians" came out to await their dis-covery. They were clad in what I imagine was the best the Sea Scouts of San Francisco could come up with, incorporating a large number of colorful chicken feathers and an impressive assortment of what appeared to be bed-room slippers. They were accompanied by a drum of sorts that most likely had been appropriated and made over from their marching band, but it gave out a satisfactory "BOOM, boom, boom, boom. BOOM, boom, boom, boom," as the "Indians" hopped from one leg to another, emitting cries of "Woo, Woo, Woo" for no apparent reason.

"Like ruptured chickens," giggled Wilson Harrison, a close Navajo friend of ours whose son Leonard was my boy Addie's best buddy and who, like Addie, was a rising star on the real competitive powwow trail. The boys, though, were more occupied in a tussle of their own than in paying much critical attention.

It was in Cy's silent grizzled stare that we could all see the smoke start-ing to rise. We could see that he regarded this "discovery" as not even "Indi-onish."

As he did every year, and would keep doing for two more decades of his life, Joe Cervetto, the owner of a local janitorial company, stepped from the mocked-up Santa Maria and waded the last few feet to shore in costumed operatic fashion. The crowd cheered as he plunged his flagstaff in the beach and the "Indians" stood in silent awe before him.

"We gotta go meet 'em," Cy said suddenly, jumping to his feet and rolling his blanket at the same time.

"Ohh, jeez," I heard Meade Chibetty groan, as if this was just what he was afraid of. The others were showing the same sort of reluctance.

"But, Cy," I said, "we don't know these people."

"C'mon!" was his only reply, and he started down the hill. Cautiously we trailed along.

It was Cy's way to instigate things, but he usually had somebody else do the talking. We straggled down the hill into the crowd of people beginning to leave the show, and I figured we probably wouldn't find anybody to talk to anyway. But Cy pulled up short all of sudden and, still staring straight ahead, waved his hand off in a direction to his right.

"Ask him," Cy told me brusquely.

He was gesturing to a sturdy, Italian-looking man with a knot of people around him who seemed to be offering their congratulations. "Ask him WHAT?" I thought, but I shrugged and started over to the little crowd, leaving my own little crowd still huddled around Cy.

That was how it started. It was the right guy, all right, the head of the Columbus Day Committee himself, and he caught my hand like a politician on election day.

"I'm Adam Nordwall," I said, fumbling to make it seem as bold and salesmanlike as possible, "and I just wanted you to know you had some real Indians watching here tonight, and . . ."

"And you want it BACK, right?" he guffawed back at me, setting off waves of laughter among his group.

You should not be any less surprised than I was to learn that the president of the Columbus Day Committee actually had a grandmother who was a Cherokee princess. Before the afternoon was out he had met each of us in turn and relayed his own kindred background. Taking me aside before he left, he assured me that if we could get it together, next year there would be real Indians there to greet Columbus.

I felt as proud as I could get relaying this information back to my friends as we headed to the wharf where our cars were parked. "He said they'll even give us fifty bucks to do it!" I announced in a capper.

"Each?" demanded Chibetty.

■

If such near pranks and what we at least saw as some new promise in fed-eral interest kept us busy and inspired at the same time, it was certainly not that easy for many, perhaps most, Indians in the Bay Area. We had reliable incomes and stable families in what I suppose should be one more category: successful suburban Indians. Others, young people especially, were pressed in the tightening vise of cities where Relocation had left them, frequently abandoned by any services at all.

La Nada Means, by her own account, had spent much of the time she worked as a barmaid in a sort of boozy haze of her own. She was a strik-ingly attractive young woman with a small child. The whirling devil of ul-timate despair that had destroyed the innocence of so many in those times could easily have absorbed her as well.

The little eastern corner of San Francisco's Mission District, where relo-cated Indians were housed in a ragged Church Street apartment house, was a mixture of dilapidated old houses squeezed among the empty warehouses and support industries of the city's dying war-time shipyards. Enough money had been scraped together to open an Indian Center in a rundown but still usable old Masonic Lodge. But the center of what was emerging as San Francisco's Little Res, as it would come to be called, was really the gloomy assortment of pool tables and loosely arranged chairs in a place called Warren's Bar, what some say was the first Indian bar in San Fran-cisco.

Had they known about it, or been clear-headed enough to give it more thought, I suppose the young Indians there would have regarded our spon-taneous deal with the Italians with bitter contempt. Anger was never far from their hearts. It was anger built of frustration with the way they had been treated by the BIA, but it was also a resentment many of them felt toward their own tribal leadership, dominated as it was by cautious older people who were corrupted, it seemed, by their long dependency on the white man. It was an anger they might have contained with the same silent rage you can still feel in towns that border reservations and feel from the Indian trade in low-down honkytonks and bars. An anger made worse by alcohol.

In the Little Res, where frustration was king and bitterness the master, there were often outbreaks of violence set off by small insults and personal slights. Young men sometimes tested each other there in displays of their own manhood and beer-flavored courage. It was also a neighborhood con-fronting transition, from the war-time period that drew blue-collar labor there (many of them Polynesian and Hispanics), to the concentration of young Indians later directed there by Relocation. Just a block from the In-dian Center was an Episcopal church known as a center for Polynesians.

The story goes that it was a couple of young brothers from the Walker River Paiute reservation in Nevada who first drew the line in what would become the turf war of the Little Res. According to the story, one of the brothers was intent on proving himself in battles with young Samoan men, themselves the pawns of similar federal promises offering opportunities to people of the "Trust Territories." Maybe it's a story confused over time. Nobody really knows if these were brothers from Walker River or from somewhere else across Indian America. They are certain, though, that tension in that neighborhood between Samoans and Indians began growing its own bitter seed in the early sixties.

San Francisco wasn't alone in having such urban problems handed to the city by Relocation. In Minneapolis, just as would occur in every Relocation center, police were especially tense and trigger-minded about Indians whom they regarded as drunks and brawlers. Police beatings were common, both during arrests and later in jail. That was how AIM, the American Indian Movement, got started. It began with patrols of young Indian men who followed the Minneapolis police, witnessing their actions, silently holding them accountable.[2]

Such AIM patrols didn't exist in San Francisco or Oakland, but the confrontations in the bars and on the street led police to use equally brutal tactics to break them up. In response, the city's Economic Opportunity Council had formed a foot patrol of its own, using young volunteers from both Indian and Samoan communities to walk the streets at night, urging peace. Al Miller was already working with the city's poverty program in the Mission District. One of their first volunteers for street patrols was Richard Oakes.

Even that, however, did little to halt the increasingly repressive police attitudes toward these "new minorities." At the United Council we began finding evidence of their actions from the news and gossip sessions that were at the heart of our weekly meetings around those squared tables. Families and friends told of many young Indian men who found themselves in San Quentin Prison almost before they realized that there was no easy escape from the pressures of the city to go "back home."

We began to visit some of the young men in prison, and we soon found that there were more of them than we realized, each caught in a more desperate and hopeless isolation than in the cities themselves.

E. E. Papke, a correctional officer (or what some called "guard" at San Quentin), had taken a special interest in the Indian prisoners. Papke was a Hawaiian, and we later inducted him into Indian America as the first honorary member of the Pineapple Tribe. He could see and sympathize with the exceptional despair experienced by Indian prisoners who were as often

Early visitor to San Quentin State Prison. The United Bay Area Council under
Adam Fortunate Eagle's leadership began annual powwows in San Quentin. *Left
to right*: E. E. Papke, San Quentin prison guard and sponsor of the American
Indian Cultural Group; Al Hicks, chairman of the Navajo Club and vice
chairman of the United Bay Area Council; Adam Fortunate Eagle; Walter
Lasley; and an associate warden of the San Quentin Prison. Photograph courtesy
of author.

counted as Caucasian or "other" in official state prison statistics, but who
were treated with continued bigotry and ignorance by the authorities.

One young Indian in prison for assault, the most common crime among
Indian convicts, had already done nearly a year in custody when he came up
for probation. Papke was there when the judge made his decision. "Well,
gee whiz," Papke recalled the judge saying, "if I put this man on probation,
I will be sending him back to his reservation in Nevada. I couldn't do that.
The conditions there are so bad, things would be better off for the man to
go to prison. He'll get good care." When Papke told that story the young
Indian was still in prison after nine years.[3]

Raymond Procunier, the head of California's Department of Correc-
tions, was an amazingly fair and understanding man for a prison boss. He
seemed willing to trust us from the beginning when I met with him and

On a cold drizzly day, Bay Area Indians enter San Quentin Prison to attend the 12th Annual Powwow of the American Indian Cultural Group, October 13, 1979. Photograph by Ilka Hartmann.

asked if we could begin a social group, even a periodic powwow, among the San Quentin Indians. To my knowledge it was the first time such a social link to the outside was permitted to Indians in any prison of the United States.

What I found at San Quentin in one way was not at all different from what we were experiencing with many young people brought in for Relocation. It was difficult for any of them, and even for some of us, to speak out on the abuses of Native Americans when they were uncertain about the laws and customs of their own people. There was a great deal we did not know about ourselves. My trips to Washington helped me understand that and led me to the odd and musty little Estates Book Store in the capital.

There I found a treasure of old publications from the nineteenth century detailing treaties, agreements, and history. The library I began building gave me enough knowledge to earn an "Eminence" credential to teach in California colleges and universities. One class I taught at Cal State–Hayward included many eager young white "wannabes." The other class, at San Quentin, was composed of Indian convicts. If it seemed to others that I was "selling out" by teaching non-Indians, it was perhaps in part because they could not see it as I did—as passing on knowledge meant to test the system.

But all of that seemed part of the rich, if tattered, fabric of what was emerging as a pan-Indian movement. The gatherings, the shows, and the powwows sponsored by the United Bay Area Council served more as a pivot than as the ultimate goal for it all. The events represented a center from which the circles expanded. In every major powwow organized in North America in those days and since, the hours after the traditional powwow dancing were always devoted to a period of socializing, sometimes well into dawn, uniquely known today among Native Americans of all tribes as a Forty-Nine.

Forty-Nines draw their origin from a group of fifty Indians from the Plains tribes who volunteered in World War I. All but one of them survived. Lacking any particular honors from the nation they served, the soldiers found distinction in singing of their exploits among their own people. A Forty-Nine is the only time you will hear English words sung (or chanted, if you like) to the drum. They are love songs for the most part, sung together by all the young people gathered around the drum. "Do I love you . . . Do I, Do I . . ." in a rhythm that almost hypnotically brings them all together. This is the time when young people feel closest to each other, and when things not permitted in a more formal powwow, such as drinking and smoking and laughing, become part of the social scene that stretches beyond traditional custom. Usually they go on all night. It was certainly well into the early morning hours when I received a call from the police complaining that one of our powwows in Hayward that summer was keeping the neighbors awake. I went to the school grounds and, as I expected to find, the Forty-Nine was still going strong. It was my responsibility, though, to keep us in good stead with the school that was letting us use their ground. It was, I also noticed, my own drum being used to keep the Forty-Nine going. When I confiscated it with as many apologies and explanations as I could, I also had some fear that I might just be asking for big trouble. Though nothing happened to me, the lead singer leveled an especially angry look in my direction. He was Al Miller.

■

I remember the first time I noticed La Nada. It wasn't La Nada herself, but a picture of her in the newspaper, crab-clinging on the back of a policeman during the Berkeley riots over Third World Studies.

La Nada had gotten herself out of the Little Res and had married one of the Means boys, with whom she would have another child, Deynon. More important, she had proved her own intelligence in making her way as a student at the University of California at Berkeley, one of the best academic institutions in the nation and, of course, at the time the broiling center of almost every student movement.

Lehman Brightman, a Sioux, had earned his master's and was teaching Native American Studies at Berkeley while he worked toward a doctorate. In some ways I guess Lehman and I were as alike as we were different. I, too, would teach Native American Studies, at Hayward State University, and he, like me, brought his knowledge to bear on issues more contemporary than historical. The difference was in approach. Lehman burned with a kind of anger that wasn't far from the streets. When he spoke of the abuses of Relocation, or of public health medical services on reservations especially, it was with a fury that gave no quarter for any white person's well-meaning intentions. To Lehman our attempts to exploit white sympathies revealed us only as fools, or worse. Lehman was more intent on exploiting the times themselves, with intense, sometimes threatening, confrontations, and there would be casualties.

La Nada, a student of Brightman's, was one of those casualties. Her all-too-obvious enthusiasm during the Third World riots brought her a suspension from the university.

How much Brightman might have sneered in contempt or even in shame at the participation of our dance group in the following year's Columbus Day event, I can only imagine. We did it to prove we were there, that Indians were not invisible or not only to be seen in the imagination of Boy Scouts. We didn't do it for the fifty bucks that Chibetty grudgingly had to accept as part of a general expense fund. We wanted more awareness of American Indians in the context of history and of the times we faced.

But in some ways we had miscalculated. The fifty bucks was about all we were getting out of it. We weren't invited to the big final banquet after the show. We weren't afforded time to express the genocidal realities that Columbus had brought with him. Only because we threatened to drop out altogether were we even permitted a place in the big Columbus Day parade through the city. We were useful in the show, but we were still made to be as invisible in reality as possible.

By 1967 we had at least pushed our own role in the landing pageant into an attention-getting performance that established Indians as more than just bit players to Columbus's show. Meade Chibetty, the big and often joking Comanche, was on the drum as the Italian committee members fidgeted over the length of the Indian performance. They could have waved at him, made some sign, even whispered in his or my ear that it was going too long. But instead one of the important Italian suits suddenly marched out from the front row and grabbed Chibetty's arm as he was drumming. That was one lucky Italian when Meade stopped and just glared at him before walking off, never to make another appearance at this show—not even when we tried to convince him for that last time in 1968.

■

"You gonna do it?" Cy said, crinkling one eye in a skeptical focus. "Are ya?"

"I'm thinking about it, Cy. Let me think about it," I said.

Joe Cervetto, the city's annual Columbus, wasn't a bad guy at all. I had become pretty good friends with the jolly little businessman, and we traded lots of jokes over the years about who really discovered whom. Cervetto had no objections to the presence we wanted in the affair, but he was a character in a pageant of his own culture. He was very proud of the role he played and of the authentically replicated Genoese costume the committee had spent $400 on to fit just him. He was, by proof of it all, "Columbus," but it was a role that really carried no influence with the Columbus Day Committee itself.

By 1968 the landing had been changed to an evening event at the marina, in part to make it easier for the ever-larger crowds who wanted to see the great reenactment climax of a weekend of Italian festivities. We played our part as usual, authentic in dress and dance for our own tribes even if we looked nothing at all like what the Taino had in 1492. The pageant had changed enough so that we actually greeted Columbus in a more ceremonial way, striding out to meet him rather than just standing in awe as the Boy Scouts had done.

"You gonna?" Cy whispered again, as Cervetto in his knee-knocking tights and bulbous apricot short pants climbed from the boat and began his ceremonious wade to shore. I strode out to meet him at the beach, carrying a coup stick cradled in one arm and thinking all the while. I let him make his symbolic stab in the sand and then put my coup stick on his shoulder as I spoke to him in a stage whisper the crowd behind me couldn't hear.

"Bend down a second, Joe, just bend down on one knee." Joe grinned at me, thinking, I suppose, that he was about to receive some kind of blessing.

As he bent down I brushed aside his floppy hat and lifted the toupee

The scalping of Joe Cervetto, San Francisco's annual Columbus, 1968.
Photograph courtesy of author.

from his head, waving it in the air. There was a gasp from the audience.
Flash cameras exploded everywhere. Joe, who had fallen down on all fours,
grinned back up at me, as good natured and as bald as ever.

We had arranged with the emcee of the event, radio disc jockey Rick
Cimino, to see the "scalping" as his cue to read a statement about the disastrous historic effects on Indians and their current presence in the Bay Area.
Cimino, who had become a friend of mine and a sympathizer with the Indian cause, did his part.

I can't be sure that everyone in the stunned crowd heard it, although I
know many of them were cheering. I'm certain that the Columbus Day
Committee was deaf with rage.

6

The Little Res

WHO WERE WE, REALLY? The Italians in San Francisco didn't know, and from that point didn't care. The general population of the Bay Area had no better idea of us than what had seemed a bizarre and colorful stunt on Alcatraz followed by the occasional small item about swarms of arrests in fights on 16th Street. Who were these Indians, anyway?

Sometimes I guess it was as hard for us to explain it to them as it was for them to understand it. We, as Indians, didn't even know each other very well at the time.

By the end of 1968, ten years after the Relocation Program first began, some estimates were that there were as many Indians living in cities as the government said were still living on reservations. That would mean there were three hundred thousand Indians concentrated for the most part in the eight cities designated as Relocation centers.[1]

No one knew for sure. The BIA Relocation Program workers who bussed young volunteers off the reservations and then ditched them within a few weeks in the forlorn pockets of new "red ghettos" made no real attempt at keeping track of them. Our guess, and it was just a guess, were that there were between fifteen and twenty thousand Indians in the Bay Area by then. Another forty thousand were estimated to be living in Los Angeles. If those figures were near the truth, then California had the second largest population of Indians in the United States. But California didn't know that. At least, officially, it acted like it didn't know it.

For all the hope and promises offered to us by the War on Poverty beginning in 1964, nothing tangible had emerged for either California tribes or urban Indians, except what we were able to do on our own. When we asked what had happened to the programs and proposals we had put forward through the Inter Tribal Council, we were politely told they were still being developed into federal policy. Years had slipped by during which the only evident policy toward Indians continued to be Termination and Relocation.

I call the Relocation Program the "Law of Unintended Consequences." What it did was to create a whole new segment of American Indians who existed aside from federal laws, apart from their own tribal laws, and at a growing distance from even their own tribal customs and cultures. That didn't assimilate them as federal authorities had hoped; it exceptionalized them into a social force the federal government had not reckoned on.

Reggie Elgin had replaced his brother Al as president of the Inter Tribal Council. Like Al, Reggie was a soft-spoken, religious kind of guy. That meant he had to reach down to find patience within himself to balance all the frustration with his personal inclination for peaceful faith. Militancy was not part of his character. Nor, I suppose, was it then a part of mine.

We had only learned indirectly through the newspaper about the series of hearings on the poverty program in California that were being chaired by Senator Robert Kennedy early in 1968. No Indians were being invited to testify. When we called the Office of Economic Opportunity asking to be included among the witnesses in San Francisco, we were told that the schedule was overbooked.

Poverty, especially then, was political. If there was one reason California didn't acknowledge the numbers of Indians in the state, it was at least in part because they carried no political clout. Farmworkers staged boycotts. Watts had already burned once, and would burn again before the year was out. Indians were known for never saying much.

Reggie and I drove to the next stop for the hearings in Sacramento. At the door we got the same excuse. It was just a half-day hearing, followed by one in the afternoon in Stockton, they explained. There just wasn't room for more testimony.

We got back in my Cadillac, but I had no intention of going home.

"We're going to Stockton, Reggie, and this time we're going to speak whether they like it or not."

They didn't, of course. "Oh, gee, no," the junior bureaucrats behind a little credentials table tried to explain. "This hearing is specifically on farm labor. You know, Hispanics. They won't be talking about Indians."

"They will if there's a bunch of us in a picket line out front when they get here!" I bluffed. It worked, though. I could see the election year wheels spinning behind the softening eyes of the committee assistant. "Uh, well, maybe, if you could be near the end maybe . . ."

I noticed him occasionally glancing at us as we sat through the bulk of the afternoon hearing. He was hoping, I think, that we'd give up and leave.

Finally our names were called, and we took seats in the witness chairs before the looming presence of Senator Robert Kennedy of New York and Senator Paul Fannin of Arizona: two non-scheduled Indians the senators' aides had not prepared them for. All the delays and stalls had at least done one thing for us—I had plenty of time to practice in my head what I was about to say.

"Senator, the United States government is our father. The state of California is our mother. And they are not married, and we are being treated accordingly. Like bastards!"

The hearing room exploded in laughter. Kennedy himself grinned with what seemed a relief of tension. For the rest of mine and Reggie's recountings of the numbers, the problems, and the frustrations, the senators listened with an ear to news they had not heard before. They were unprepared with any of the usual political responses and uncertain of even what questions to ask us.

When it was over and the hearing was ending, Kennedy sent over an aide to ask us to meet him backstage. Those few brief moments when the potential president congratulated us and probed for a little more specific information were just about the only real success I can remember having with the War on Poverty. I felt a little better after just shaking his hand. Within two months the Inter Tribal Council had received its first grant of a quarter million dollars to aid California rancherias. At that point, done with my work and conscious of my place as part of a non-California tribe, I turned over the money and resigned with pride.

I saw Robert Kennedy once more. It was during his election campaign and he was making a visit to the San Francisco Indian Center. Two weeks later he was shot to death in Los Angeles.

There was chaos in America that year. The assassination of Martin Luther King Jr. had set cities ablaze. In the Bay Area, and especially in Oakland where the Black Panther Party had formed and almost immediately been attacked by police, riots were expected but never came. That was perhaps because the Panthers and other organizations like them found the Bay Area to be a uniquely accepting place of emerging new political thought. The "Summer of Love" and all the hippies in the Haight Ashbury had only begun the year before. Students were active everywhere in the growing protests against the war in Vietnam. It was a year to be young in the Bay Area. Even in the Little Res.

■

Alan Miller grew up on the Seminole Reservation in Laney, Oklahoma. White Americans are often confused by that. They envision Seminoles as slipping through the mangroves and snake-infested forests of Florida, not as subsisting on the dry plains of Oklahoma. But it was the fate of the Seminoles to have first been pushed south from their native homes, deeper and deeper into the Everglades and, finally, when they would not surrender even there, to follow other tribes in the grim marches east to Indian Territory in Oklahoma. Al was a full-blood Indian, from a powerful tradition of courage and initiative. When he was seventeen he joined the U.S. Marine Corps and served on active duty for more than five years until 1966. Back home, on the reservation, all the BIA had to offer him was Relocation. Al chose San Francisco and the Little Res around the Mission District's 16th Street.

He described what he found there as a kind of shock therapy: "I had already been in the Marine Corps and seen some of the world," he told an interviewer. "I was a little more hip than most of the Indians that were sent out from the reservation. I'm not exaggerating, there were guys who didn't know quite how to cross the street yet. They would wait for people to cross and they'd cross with them."[2]

For all his experience, Al found the Relocation Program no more useful to him than it had been to others. He was soon "cut loose," as he described it, and left in the city hanging around the Indian Center, going to the Friday night dances there, and looking for the kinship many other young Indians were finding just next door at Warren's Bar.

The bartender, only recently arrived himself from New York, was an enthusiastic young Mohawk named Richard Oakes.

Much of Richard's early background remains fuzzy. People said he told them he had worked in high steel, but it was a media-promoted cliché of those times that Mohawks were somehow uniquely suited to the daring heights of skyscraper construction. Others thought Richard just let them assume that about him. Richard's wife, Anne, has never talked to reporters or writers about it. Anne is a Pomo from Stewart's Point, California, and it seems certain she met and married Richard while he was a first-year student at San Francisco State University.

From their first meeting at Warren's, Al was impressed by Richard. He had what Al saw as a charismatic style, a natural sense of leadership combined with almost reckless enthusiasm, and seemed willing to take on anybody, including the cops. Whether or not he had ever balanced himself on a narrow beam above a city, to Al Richard seemed fearless enough to do it. They faced some grim streets together, and Al became Richard's closest friend and his most loyal lieutenant.

A year that witnessed so many national tragedies seemed too full of agony to give much notice when Clyde Warrior died. Almost without question, Warrior was regarded as the most promising and popular young Indian activist of his time. He emerged almost as an icon for a new movement, and yet he died before it could take shape. He was on his way home to Oklahoma from Los Angeles. Authorities said he succumbed to alcoholism.

Like La Nada Means did in her way, Richard and Al soon straddled two significant continents in the emerging world of urban Indians. On one side was the rapidly forming Native American Studies group at San Francisco State, which was then being organized by a quietly efficient academic named Gerald Sams. Richard, almost with Al in tow, took an active part, citing his own experience as a member of the ambitiously envisioned traveling university that had been proposed by the White Roots of Peace, a vaguely Native American group formed on the East Coast and traveling, almost hippie-like, to various campuses with its spiritual message of creating new standards of education based on models of the Iroquois Federation—the six tribes that included Richard's own Mohawk ancestors.[3]

There was stimulation and inspiration to be found in the flood of academic discussions that absorbed even freshman classes at San Francisco State and elsewhere in the search for new knowledge. And always there was the other foot that the two friends, Richard and Al, and dozens of other young Indians like them, kept at least lightly planted in places like the Little Res. It was there in the honky-tonk melody and blue evening bravado that you would find the sort of spirit and daring that gave definition to all the academic talk. Joe Bill, an Eskimo, or Inuit, was there, wound up tight like an electric motor ready to go whenever the power was turned on. Ross Harden was there, and Cyril Lefthand, and others just waiting for the right words that could channel their energy into something better than just battling the cops on Friday nights.

These were parallel universes: mine and that of the United Council; Lehman Brightman and his UC–Berkeley influence; the Sioux Club (which still held the council at a distance) and the combination of students and street people defined, somehow, as the Little Res. These groups were parallel—thinking similar things, coming up with similar conclusions—but they were not converging, and there seemed nothing ahead that would draw them into a single focus.

■

In April 1969 another hearing was held that in some ways proved to be conclusive. It was convened by the National Council on Indian Opportunity, nominally chaired by Vice President Spiro Agnew, but actually run by LaDonna Harris and her Committee on Urban Indians. LaDonna is a Comanche who even by then had compiled an admirable insider's reputation for dealing with Washington politics. (Her husband, Senator Fred Harris, was one of the most influential members of Congress.) The committee included five other Indians selected as a cross section of tribal affairs in the United States. Purely a fact-finding forum, the hearing produced nothing more in practical solutions than any of the others had. But its impact was seen in the Bay Area group that was assembled to testify.

Earl Livermore, the eloquent and practical-minded head of the San Francisco Indian Center, was there. So was Rupert Costo of the American Indian Historical Society, and David Risling of the California Indian Education Association, both of them acknowledged scholars on California Native Americans. Richard McKenzie was there, strongly supported by a Sioux group that included Stella Leach. Lehman Brightman made an appearance and, of course, so did I, along with E. E. Papke from our San Quentin group.

By then I was better prepared than ever to address not only the issues but the background of mistreatment and bigotry that plagued our people. My experience with the War on Poverty may not have brought much action from Washington, but it had led me steadily into more and more research. From trips to the capital and elsewhere I had compiled a library of my own numbering over five hundred books, many of them rare government volumes.

But beyond those of us who could claim academic knowledge, Harris's committee had also invited people from the street, people who knew firsthand about our grievances. People like Horace Spencer, who told of the disastrous things Relocation had done to his family. And for the first time that I know about, there was official recognition of Indian students in the Bay Area, represented by Richard Oakes of San Francisco State.

I can't say that Richard was impressive in this, his first really public appearance. He shyly stumbled into a short statement, setting off laughter when he said that the Native American Studies Program would provide better understanding to social workers. "Social workers need badly trained Indians," he said, juggling the words.[4] But in his brief statement Richard did characterize the rising sense among Indian students wanting to be recognized for their own heritage and, although he did not say so directly, often undereducated about how it counted in their own lives.

Far beyond Richard, though, was the expression of that spirit among students delivered by Mary Lou Justice, a classmate of Richard and Al's at State and a close friend of theirs in the Little Res. Mary Lou's story was close to that of La Nada's. She was a young woman with a small child, apart from her own reservation, confronting and unwilling to accept an uncertain future.

"I know who I am," she said. "I'm an Indian. But will my children? They won't feel the same love for the land or the reservation that I do, and so we're going to have a generation that doesn't know who they are or where they belong."[5]

Her testimony about nearly starving herself in the city and finding her way through dead-end jobs and finally into college was riveting and drew waves of applause. She, especially, should have been better remembered from that day.

My own testimony was, admittedly, long and involved as Papke and I went through the injustices visited upon Indians both in prison and on the streets. Dick McKenzie, who had testified earlier in a brief statement stressing the lack of news media attention to urban Indians, seemed to grow more uncomfortable the longer my appearance went on.

"You've been testifying for forty-five minutes now," he blurted out from the audience at one point. I had, it was true, but most of it had been in answer to questions from Harris's committee. What irritated McKenzie most, apparently, was my mention of some Indians, such as W. W. Keeler of Phillips Petroleum, who had expressed interest in the cause of urban Indians and gotten virtually nowhere in finding a way to focus it even from his seat on the board of a rich oil company.[6]

As always, McKenzie wanted action, but had only a vague notion of what form that action should take beyond his demanding style. Stella Leach put forth the increasingly difficult problems of providing health care for urban Indians, especially the children. Others spoke of poor housing, indifferent social workers, ignorant teachers.

Lee Brightman's name had been called twice in the first session and once again on the second day. Finally, sometime during that mid-morning he showed up, burr-cut from head down, demanding to be heard as if a soldier from the street.

"This is no better than the Bureau of Indian Affairs," he thundered, and he could sense the awakening his hostility had roused from the crowd. "They are made up predominantly of white people; they constantly want to survey us and hear our problems; and now you come down and tell us you can't do anything; you've got to convince them in Washington there are Indians in urban areas, and you hole up in one of the richest hotels in the United States. I think this is just peachy-keen; this is a typical survey!"[7]

San Francisco's Sheraton Palace might have been one of the richest hotels in the United States when President Warren G. Harding died there, but by 1969 it was more of a fading remnant of better times on Market Street. Still, Brightman, in his customary style of attacking the symbols of white man's domination, knew he was on a roll. For the rest of the hearing there were eruptions of mild protests, fueled in part by his confrontational style. McKenzie complained loudly of "opportunist" Indians. Somebody suggested the city hadn't even bothered to send the Tac Squad of police that usually attended Indian gatherings such as those near Warren's Bar. Even the scholarly David Risling questioned the good of yet one more hearing going nowhere. Frustration was showing, not just with federal inaction but with what we could all begin to see was a lack of unity among ourselves and a shortage of clear leadership for our young people.

Near the very end of the two days of hearings it was Brightman himself who suggested in another long outburst that we, in his words, "bury the hatchet."

"We can be the only area in the whole United States that is totally organized," he said, "and if an Indian is in trouble he can go to any of these organizations and get help. And if any of these organizations need help we will all back them. This business of name calling in public and name calling each other and criticizing each other and criticizing each organization, the intertribal, and so forth, we've got to stop."

There was applause that faded out along with the hearing. The year 1969 had only just begun.

7

Alert the Media

BOBBIE AND I HAD NO REASON to expect that we would ever again hear from the young VISTA representative who so abruptly seemed to end his government career in that Chinatown bar. So I was surprised when Tim Findley telephoned our home in 1968 to say he had been hired as a reporter for the *San Francisco Chronicle*.

"Alright!" I responded, perhaps a little less restrained in my enthusiasm than I should have been. But if there was one thing I thought we needed to be able to get beyond the plodding indecision of Washington, it was a sympathetic press. Findley was still only twenty-four and a "cub" reporter at best on the region's dominant morning newspaper, but he was no doubt a friend and someone who understood at least a little about Indians. In fact, while working at a Denver radio station he had become a frequent confidant of Vine Deloria and supporter of Vine's "Custer campaign."

Tim was still something of a rebel, though, always at odds with his bosses at a time when rebellion claimed its special status. I had already pestered the *Chronicle* and other newspapers in recent years with repeated attempts to win free publicity for our powwows and our social attempts among prisoners, especially. Tim tried too, but usually met with little more success than I had myself in convincing the editors that there was an Indian population worth noticing in the Bay Area. Even for that informational hearing before LaDonna Harris's committee the newspapers and the media in general had elected not to assign any coverage.

Findley, however, made his way in establishing a niche of his own in *Chronicle* coverage, first by reporting on the trial of Black Panther cofounder Huey Newton, and later by winning more and more trust among radical student leaders of the so-called New Left. By the summer of 1969 he

Alcatraz Island in the San Francisco Bay. Photograph by Brooks Townes.

was being promoted by fellow staff members as a Pulitzer Prize candidate for his coverage of Berkeley's People's Park riots.

If that coverage might have been insignificant to us at the time, it later proved to be a crucial, and controversial, gear in what was gradually beginning to mesh as an Indian movement.

Lee Brightman's sound for unity at the Harris hearings still held only hollow promise, for it lacked something that could bring all the various organizations and purposes among Indians into some kind of harmony. Only the year before, at the 1968 confirmation hearings for Interior Secretary Walter Hickel, Lee and I had confronted each other in a nearly violent exchange over my moderate approach to "educate" the nominee and the Senate committee on abuses of Alaskan Native Americans, which was in conflict with Lee's always more blunt approach, which he characterized as "Pickle Hickel." Ours was more than just a difference in style. It was almost a campaign between us to establish leadership among the shattered interests of Indian people in the Bay Area.

Searching for a focus, looking in our way for something that might give us the kind of identity that was so insistently obvious among blacks and students, we were frequently drawn in our discussions at the United Council to the unresolved issue of Alcatraz.

McKenzie's efforts, and those of the Sioux, to claim exclusive rights under the Black Hills Treaty, had been discredited in the courts and, more than that, had lost favor among the broadly pan-tribal group that saw our cause more and more as "Indian" rather than tribal.

Still, Alcatraz, the American "Devil's Island," sulked out there in the Bay, abandoned by all but a series of former prison officials who served as caretakers and who guarded it from visits by curiosity seekers who had no better idea than anybody else about what to do with the Rock.

When at last the federal General Services Administration announced that the surplus island property would be offered to the city of San Francisco for whatever best use they could find for it, we on the council began toying with the idea of making our own bid. We passed this idea around the table for everybody to examine and think about. Some didn't want to offend the Sioux by taking over what had, after all, been their idea to start with. Others didn't see there could be much to gain from acquiring the cold and desolate piece of a notorious past. Still others saw it as perhaps symbolic enough to claim just a part of it and establish that, maybe, as a kind of western beacon of Native Americans, something like the Statue of Liberty in New York Harbor.

There was talk that Alcatraz could be remodeled somehow and brought up to date as a center for cultural preservation and education but, really, I don't think any among us at that point thought such an ambitious plan was truly practical. We joked that it was, in general, a pretty useless and barren piece of property in an otherwise spectacular place. Something like an Indian reservation.

Give credit to ketchup and simple feminine influence for what happened next. Lamar Hunt, son of the Texas produce tycoon H. L. Hunt, offered to the San Francisco Board of Supervisors what they saw as the only financially viable plan they had heard. Hunt wanted to convert the island into a kind of adult amusement park, as gaudy and as close to a Las Vegas image as the current law would permit. The supervisors gave their preliminary approval, but San Francisco dress designer Alvin Duskin, who had invented the A Line skirt that made his reputation, blew up in a well-financed fury of his own. He bought big ads in the papers pounding at the "crass" and "tasteless" idea of turning Alcatraz over to the Texas entrepreneur and called upon sophisticated citizens to protest such debasement. Underneath Duskin's outrage, but generally understood in San Francisco, was revulsion for Hunt's notoriously right-wing politics that were totally out of step with the direction in which the city was headed. As much as Duskin and others resented the idea of making a glitzy eyesore of Alcatraz, they also rejected the thought of giving Hunt a toehold in city policy.

We were wide-eyed. This was a battle of big bucks over the future of a little island where we had been told only five years before, "if you want it, you can have it."

"Why not?" Chibetty said at our meeting. "I mean, if they're going to fight over it, why don't we give them some way to get out of the whole thing?"

So I did. I called John Barbagelata, who was a member of the San Francisco Board of Supervisors and somebody I had met on a couple of occasions. Like much of the city's current leadership he was Italian, and far more conservative than those who saw a different future for the city.

"What?" he said, as if not hearing me the first time.

"It could be a good thing, Supervisor, and solve all your problems with this stuff. We'd give you $24 in beads or something, like they did for New York, and you could turn it over to us. Then, you know, we'd get federal help for an Indian center and maybe a college . . ."

"Oh, uh, look Adam," he said. "I know what you're saying, and we'll certainly take it into consideration. You know, we haven't really decided anything yet, but, well, we'd just have to look at that very closely."

Okay, I didn't record the call or take notes or anything, but near as I can remember after all these years, that was how it went. San Francisco's city fathers at the time had their chance from the beginning.

■

I just can't recall exactly how Richard Oakes and I got to know each other after that hearing with LaDonna Harris, but I know for sure that as chairman of the United Bay Area Council in Oakland I called Don Patterson of the San Francisco Indian Center to tell him of our discussions about Alcatraz. There was an even more important reason for that, and I think, probably, that's what brought Richard into the discussions.

Warren's Bar, the emerging Native American Studies group at State, even the Psychology 101 class where Al Miller remembers first discussing with Richard and Mary Lou Justice the symbolism of Alcatraz, could not by themselves have triggered the student interest.[1] Neither, for that matter, could I. It would require one of those balmy warm evenings in early autumn that characterize the contrary climate of San Francisco. In the Little Res a new college semester had begun to diminish the summertime enthusiasm of students still forming their new curriculums. From the classrooms of spring into the streets of summer there had come some new ideas and new translations, but with the start of a new season the late night's intellectual energy was slipping back like fog into the coastal hills where San Francisco State was housed.

For many years to come there were suspicions about who was responsible for the fire that destroyed the San Francisco Indian Center on October 10th. Among the young Indians close to the Mission District, it was rumored that the Samoans were the perpetrators, which added to the long rivalry. But Al Miller and others, who came back to the question again and again, concluded later that most likely it was two Indians themselves, too drunk to remember what they were doing, who set off the fire.

Now that "other foot" on which the San Francisco State students like Al and Richard and Mary Lou had stood took on even more meaning. Richard may not have quickly distinguished between opportunity and disaster, but from his place in Warren's Bar he could not have missed the confusion that searched for some new answer. He has been described in many romantic and exaggerated ways since then, but fundamentally Richard was far more of a gentle dreamer than he ever was an impassioned politician. His dreams, founded in part by what he had learned from White Roots of Peace, drifted into images not only of new education but of radically impossible-sounding new ideas. He envisioned new fields of aquaculture, of literally growing strawberries beneath the Bay. He saw Indians reclaiming not just the wilderness of their own lands, but the wealth of it, all coming together in an organized process that would stem from a single great think tank of new ways, someplace apart from government and corporate restrictions on thought, a place where all the old obligations would no longer apply. These were exuberant (some might say sophomoric) dreams, but they blended with the times, and Richard flung them out like spears.

"A girl named Mary Lou Justice," Al Miller would recall many years later. "She had the original idea of taking Alcatraz, and in that classroom we kicked it around. . . . And Richard was in that class and he kind of emerged as the leader because he had a lot of guts and a lot of vision for things. He had a lot of weird ideas, you know, ocean farming. Some of his famous words were things like, 'we can use this as a catalyst to get off into other things, to claim other land and start other movements.'"

If, perhaps, Al's admiration of Richard was even stronger in later years than at the time, and thus condensed in memory, it's still fair to recognize that the Sioux occupation of Alcatraz, however brief, had established a thought in the minds of many of us. A thought running parallel in all our minds, but, until the San Francisco Indian Center burned, still lacking a point.

■

It was a relatively small item written from the police beat in the morning papers. An old building, used by Indians as a meeting hall, had been destroyed in a fire of undetermined origin. Losses were estimated as purely monetary.

Tim Findley tried to discover the fire's origin, but he was absorbed in battles of his own with his bosses over coverage of two massive antiwar demonstrations planned for the next month in San Francisco. A young police beat reporter, John Leaning, actually went to the Mission District and interviewed Al Miller and other Indians, but the reporter was only able to call in notes to his city desk, which never appeared as a full story. The heart of the Little Res had been destroyed without the public even knowing of its existence.

Once again, I tried making a case to the San Francisco Board of Supervisors. This time I had the backing of Earl Livermore and Don Patterson, as well as others, in suggesting that the city had an excellent opportunity to solve two problems at once: Alcatraz, and the replacement of the Indian Center.

"I gotta give you credit, Adam," laughed Supervisor Barbagelata. "You do persist. It's just something we'll have to consider, that's all."

Just "taking it," as we had done before, occurred to us, and made even more sense the longer we were put off by official circles. But who would do it? Would it be the Sioux again, in what was certain to be a self-limiting act? Could we all claim it as being owed to California Native Americans in general? Could we just "take it" the same way lands had been taken from all of us? We talked about these questions at the United Council in Oakland. But the crisis the fire brought to the San Francisco group prompted a more urgent need. As the representative of our council, I presented the idea to Livermore and others in a meeting at the temporary headquarters that the San Francisco Indian Center had found in an old glass-walled storefront about the size of a five and dime. Although it lacked chairs and certain other comforts, it had plenty of space that was gradually filled with standing crowds as those discussions went on during warm mid-October evenings.

No matter what may have been written or said, the plan we formed was not the idea of "militants" or "radicals" any more renegade than my suburban self. McKenzie had moved on to a War on Poverty job in Washington State. Chalk Cottier was content with letting the meetings find their own way. Brightman, churning out angry slogans and vaguely racist threats from his "War Path" publication in Berkeley, wanted nothing to do with staging another "event" at Alcatraz. Brightman sneered at the notion, telling me he would "hold my coat" while we took on "the establishment" in such a way. To him it would be clownish and insignificant. AIM and the National Indian Youth Council, though active in the Midwest, had no real presence at all in the Bay Area, and nothing at all to do with our discussion or our ultimate plan for the capture of the Rock.

It was really in that slightly seedy Mission District storefront that an alliance began to grip together the past and the future in a way that none of us could have envisioned. The new vision was clearly distinct from what some have imagined since was a Berkeley theme in the action. Al Miller and Richard Oakes and, I suppose, Mary Lou Justice, stood impatiently among the crowd, knowing it should soon be their turn to lead. I had seen the change in leadership coming too, especially since the hearings earlier that year. The students at Berkeley felt themselves closer to Brightman, but he was having problems with a younger group challenging his leadership. The situation had gone so far that, according to rumor, Brightman had suggested to his wife that she take a swing at Henrietta Whiteman of the opposition group. That, at least, was the tale told with laughter at the Friendship House. The students, the young people in general from the Little Res, saw themselves more urgently involved in an issue of their own. I was not just taking an opportunity by beginning to recognize and recruit Richard as their leader. The initiative was a practical step that obviously would be necessary to bring together the support we needed from young people. They were establishing their own way. They might join, but they no longer would be so easily led by elders as they had in the past. Richard and I talked, uncertain of trust at first, but with growing respect for each other. I loaned him some books (the report from the Hickel hearing in particular), and we began to get to know each other. It helped, I think, that I had already established a relationship with other members of Annie Oakes's Pomo tribe who were affiliated with the United Council.

Findley's efforts to find an "angle" that would help him sell the story of the center had also led him to Richard and Annie. Annie was supportive of her husband in a quiet way. They were raising five young kids on Richard's bartending salary and his high hopes from college. Ruggedly, romantically handsome Richard portrayed himself as balancing the needs of family and cause; he tried, seriously, to carry them all on his shoulders at once. I think the instincts of any reporter would be to watch that drama play out.

For her own reasons, La Nada, too, saw what was evolving from the talk about the island as a gesture that defined her own frustrations, even if it meant breaking from Brightman and his UC–Berkeley allegiance.

Just talking about Alcatraz, whether the discussion took place in the United Council or during a psychology class at State or in Warren's Bar, would never take us beyond a place where we had been stalled so often before. A rerun of the "show" in 1964 would only confirm the doubts of

Brightman and others about our actions having any real meaning at all. The more we talked the more we realized that this time we would have to take a serious stand. I told Tim Findley in a telephone call that we were intending to do it. I wanted to know how he thought the media would respond.

"You kidding?" he said. "You're gonna grab it like they grabbed the (People's) park? Berkeley in the Bay? It'll be a massacre!"

Nevertheless, Findley's judgment was that if enough press was around, at least a point could be made. He told me that he was planning a Halloween party at his new house in Sausalito that had a gorgeous hillside view of the Bay. There would be an assortment of all his friends, including Black Panthers, student radicals, rising liberal political leaders of San Francisco, and, of course, lots of other reporters mingling in what he had established as a sort of free zone where nobody got quoted.

"If you want," he said, "that would be one hell of a time to bring it up. One thing, though. If it wouldn't be too much trouble, do you think you could pick up Richard and Annie on the way?"

■

Bobbie and I drove across the Bay Bridge, then south along the city, heading in a long loop that would stop first at the cluster of apartments and old Quonset huts that formed the San Francisco State married student housing quarters they still called "Gatorville." Richard wanted to be at the party as a representative of the students and, I suspect, as a moderating influence on what they still suspected was the United Council's and my own "older" ideas. Annie, always shy among new people, reluctantly joined her frequently unpredictable husband as we headed north across the Golden Gate to Sausalito.

Tim's house was stuck on a steep hillside facing south. Just getting to the door required negotiating a curving set of stone stairs that plunged down from the street. Inside, though, it commanded a glittering view of San Francisco and the entire Bay before it. There in the center was Alcatraz, like a huge blunt-bowed yacht run aground, its lighthouse beacon sweeping across the dark water in a steadily rotating pattern. The Dutch door entrance to Tim's house was open at the top, and we invited ourselves in to a swirling crowd of music and conversation that seemed to lack any obvious direction or organization. Such costumes and masks as might be appropriate for Halloween were sophisticated but generally put aside in the unrestrained mingle.

But that was the way those parties went. Tim's idea was just to mix as many different people together as possible, stir lightly with plenty of free drinks, and see what would happen. He and his wife, Marilyn, were generous hosts, eager to make everybody as comfortable as possible, but there was some sociology going on there, too. We were introduced to a group at a time in the clusters of conversations—Earl Caldwell of the *Times*, Mike Mills of KRON TV, David Lawday from Reuters . . . and over there was Blake Green from the *Chronicle*, Jack Smith who covered the Raiders, the guy from *Newsweek* who was talking to Panther Chief of Staff David Hilliard. We were sort of just being tossed into the salad, and I can't really blame Richard for the way he concentrated mostly on the view and his brandy glass. Annie huddled close to him, as if trying somehow to disappear in the shadows.

There were politicians there, too—the up-and-coming ones who were part of the times. Among them were Terry Hallinan, who would become the district attorney of San Francisco but was then the organizer of the New Mobilization March Against the War that soon put 250,000 people on San Francisco streets, and Willie Brown, just then beginning a career that rapidly took him to leadership of the California State Assembly and eventually to be mayor of San Francisco.

They all swapped insider jokes the way reporters and politicians always do in social settings, and even if my own ever-public personality fit in fairly well, I could see that Richard was feeling awkward. Tim had said this would be a good time to announce our plan, but I couldn't see how that crowd could possibly be focused into one party-stopping statement by anybody.

"Just wait, Adam," he said. "They're talking about Hunt and Duskin and all that, it's bound to get to you."

It did. It was somewhere in the kitchen, I think, where there was a barrelful of flavored apples, when, at some point that crazy, cusswording thing with Hunt was leading to more and more one-liners about Alcatraz. Satisfied that he could see a focus, Tim loudly proclaimed, "Adam has the AN-SWER!" He looked at me and said, "Go for it."

You need to keep in mind that at least some of the reporters had seen me before during all my pestering efforts to win coverage of Indian events. They expected me to be something of a PR man. They didn't know what to think of Richard.

"Well, we're going to take it back," I began, to the accompanying laughter. "No, I mean it. We already have a plan to occupy Alcatraz as a new Indian center." The convivial laughter was fading out. This, everyone knew, was no news conference, and what got said wasn't meant for publication, but I was suggesting something with trouble attached.

I didn't make a long announcement or speech, just a sort of statement I would repeat again and again as the night went on, that so long as nobody blew it in advance, we'd tip them off when we were ready to make our move. Chances are most of the reporters figured their editors wouldn't be interested anyway, but they all agreed to hold the "news" for our move. It was Tim, more than me, I think, who took special notice of the fact that none of the politicians there raised any objections to the idea. But it was I, far more than Tim, who could see from his suddenly gregarious conversations that we definitely had Richard on board.

It was like putting a new record on the party stereo. From that point on there was a theme in the conversations that, with rising volume and his sometimes fantastic solo ideas, included Richard.

Unfortunately, Richard became quite drunk. Well, at least as drunk as the sportswriter he started arguing with, to the point that they seemed about to trade blows. We had to steady Richard a little as we climbed back up the stone steps to the street.

Richard, after all, was new to this business. Not new to parties, perhaps, or even to city people, but he was new to the attention of people who might have influence and who might instinctively be sizing him up for what influence he might have. Despite the little fight, he had come away pretty well and established himself as someone they would remember.

We talked about that going across the Golden Gate Bridge in the early morning dark with Richard and Annie riding in the back seat of the Cadillac. As we reached 19th Avenue heading back toward Gatorville, Richard said he wasn't feeling well.

Maybe some did think our car was a little too showy for an Indian and his cause, but I was glad that night I could electronically control the back seat window so Annie could help Richard lean out into the passing air.

8

Voyage of the *Monte Cristo*

IN WASHINGTON, D.C., THERE WAS EVIDENCE that at least some of our message had gotten through. The newly elected Nixon administration, bogged down from the start in a highly unpopular war that threatened to open even larger fractures in American society, did not want the burden of still more disputes over domestic policy.

President-elect Nixon formally offered to end Termination as a policy objective of his administration in return for some sort of greater "self-determination" of the tribes in "planning their own destiny."[1]

Nixon's Interior Secretary, former Alaska governor Walter Hickel, had been battered in the Senate confirmation hearings over the treatment of Alaskan Natives. Robert Bennett, an enrolled member of the Oneida Tribe, had served as Commissioner of Indian Affairs during the final years of the Johnson administration, and was known as an opponent to the old policy of Termination which, though less actively pursued, was still the "sense of Congress." Nixon dropped Bennett from his sub-cabinet. On the Oneida reservation in Wisconsin there was growing concern that the tribe might be next on the "Doomsday Book" for Termination.

On October 8, 1969, only two days before the San Francisco Indian Center burned down, Hickel told a meeting of the National Congress of American Indians that among "many needs" was the need to create a way for Indians to speak with one voice. "The challenge to meet the needs is ours—yours and mine," he said. "I can help. But in the final analysis, the future of the Indians—America's first citizens—must be shaped by the Indians, for the Indians."[2]

There was much too much going on by then for us to be distracted by yet another vague and florid promise from the great white father. But Hickel would get his chance to stand by his words.

The Halloween party had been only a little break in the frenetic pace of meetings and planning sessions, telephone calls, and growing lists of contacts that were commanding all our attention. The party had, however, accomplished two important objectives: we had established an important core group among the media who would at least understand what was behind the action, and Richard had put himself forth as being willing, as I put it to him, to "carry the ball" for what was to come next.

The students had a particular problem with the urgency of the timing. It was not even mid-semester yet. There had hardly been time enough to contact all those returning to various campuses, let alone organize them, for an action that would disrupt their academic standing far more than some demonstration planned around the more customary time of spring break or at least during the Christmas holidays. But we could not wait. All the wheels were in motion. The federal government wanted to unload the island to the city of San Francisco. The city was fighting itself over Hunt's offer, and the temporary headquarters for the Indian Center could not sustain the energy needed to support some dramatic move. Now added to all this was the tip-off to the media, and its notoriously short attention span.

Bit by bit the Alcatraz idea had taken hold with growing enthusiasm. In meetings people cited conditions on their own reservations or their own experiences with Relocation as evidence for the cause. Alcatraz was run down and isolated, as were many reservations. It had no source of water. There were plenty of places "back home" where people remembered having to haul water in barrels. No health care. No transportation. No heat in the winter. All familiar problems.

I found myself making more and more trips to the Scientific Analysis Corporation on California Street in San Francisco, where our friend and the quiet benefactor of many Indian causes, Dr. Dorothy (Lone Wolf) Miller, had the technical facilities to put what we were discussing into a more organized form. We needed to make our reasons clear to as many people as possible. Using the proposal offered by the United Council in 1968 as a foundation, Dorothy and I started restructuring it into what she suggested should be a "proclamation" that would contain some of the satire and humor that was part of our discussions. "Indians of All Tribes" was added as the authority for what became our "document of discovery."

Richard was busy with making contacts of his own. Just for the sake of the numbers we needed, let alone the demonstration of wide support we wanted, we needed to look beyond the Mission District and San Francisco State alone. Despite her troubles with the university over it, La Nada had become the only Indian (and the only woman) on the negotiating commit-

A prison island. Photograph by Ilka Hartmann

tee for the student Third World Council at Berkeley. Something of what she had learned from that experience was reflected in the language she used recalling her telephone discussion with Richard at this time.

"I was on [the Berkeley] campus when I got a call from Richard, and he said Adam Nordwall was going to rent a boat and go around the island," she recalled, perhaps a little imperfectly, in reconstructing our planned intentions. "We were pretty upset with the fact that we'd been ignored on the reservations, the fact that our people were still being held as political prisoners, socially, economically, and politically."[3]

Infused with vintage Berkeley "political prisoner" rhetoric or not, La Nada signed on to our cause from that moment with a warrior's spirit that would burn brighter and last longer than any of the other young people from the campuses and the city streets who found inspiration in the idea. Hers was a special energy, at the very sharp edge of her time in what, even on the Berkeley campus, was only just beginning as a militant women's movement.

We were committed. There would be no turning back.

"A-Day" to reclaim the island was set for Sunday, November 9.

■

In my mind this point in time was the only near-perfect window we had. Charlie Manson's "family" was being rounded up in Los Angeles to sensational coverage, but this was tabloid stuff. There was a break between the waves of huge demonstrations against the war. The press was quoting speeches by Vice President Spiro Agnew which, to me, had to indicate they needed something better to fill the space. Sunday fit with the unusual joint printing agreement of San Francisco's two major papers, which granted the lower-circulating afternoon *Examiner* exclusive Sunday news production but almost guaranteed longer feature space in the Monday morning *Chronicle*. One good Sunday story was almost certain to have what the reporters called "legs" to last over two or three more days. I played it as carefully as I could, alerting only the *Chronicle* and Mike Mills of KRON, along with a couple of others I knew we could trust, before the weekend began. The rest I planned to phone on Saturday.

Back in my bowling days, and even for some time after that, I was also a pretty fair fisherman. I had my own sea pole that I took with me on frequent trips aboard the party boats out under the Golden Gate into the salmon runs. I knew some of the boat owners, the ones who worked with the outfit "Jerry's" on Fisherman's Wharf in particular. Beyond that, flashy Jack LaRue in his time had introduced me to the owners of the Grotto Restaurant in Oakland's Jack London Square. I became good friends with them, and relied on their knowledge of which boats were capable of taking out fishing groups.

Five boat owners, six if you counted the questionable seaworthiness of the vessel owned by Papke's brother, agreed to ferry the party I avoided describing as "invaders" out to Alcatraz.

It was chaotic, the details and logistics demanding and distracting all at once, but it seemed to be coming together. By Thursday we had settled on a final draft of the Proclamation, and Dr. Miller was printing out copies of it for us. "Ten A.M. on Sunday," I told Richard and the others, hoping that detail wouldn't be shaded too much by notoriously late "Indian time."

Bobbie and I, of course, were among those who found last-minute details were standing in the way of our own schedule. It was already just after 10:00 when we arrived at the open pier. Papke was there waiting, wearing a worried, slightly frantic look on his face.

"They're not here, Adam," the big Hawaiian said. "None of them have shown up."

Pier 39 on the eastern rim of Fisherman's Wharf was not then the busy shopping mall and strolling dock it is today. In those days it was just another long board finger out into the Bay left generally unused since the end of World War II when the city lost its trade with cruise ships. Sunday morning on the wharf is generally still ahead of the tourist crowds, and this was November anyway. There was a stomach-turning emptiness to it all.

"Don't worry, don't worry," I said. "They'll be here." Papke's own boat had suffered a crunching collision the night before. At least I knew it wouldn't be coming. "They're just late, that's all," I tried to reassure him.

I recognized some of the media already milling around like they were looking for a place to set up their shots. Other Indians were arriving in groups at a time, thank goodness, living up to their reputation for not paying too much attention to the clock.

My own group from the East Bay had followed our inclination to put forward as much of a traditional presence as possible. Many were outfitted in tribal dress with fringed shawls and buckskin, beaded vests, and bright shirts. Some, including me, wore at least parts of dance outfits (like my own flower-beaded yoke and porcupine quill roach), and others had an assortment of stunning feather bustles, some of the youngsters especially.

These were in contrast to the more drab and restrained street garb of the young people from San Francisco and Berkeley. There was a broad flat-billed reservation hat here or there, a headband, a belt buckle, some neck beads, but they obviously did not come dressed for a "show" and there was, perhaps, some instinctive difference in how we grouped—like people who didn't get the same invitation to a party.

But somebody, Al Miller I think, had brought a drum, and the thrumming rhythm that drew the dancers and singers to it was at least a diversion for the media.

No boats. I tried not to be obvious about it as I looked up and down the rows of piers for some sign of them. I wanted it to seem that I was only symbolically preparing myself by gazing out toward Alcatraz, but secretly I was scanning the water. No boats.

In the corner of my eye I could see Findley was watching. I knew what he was thinking: Indian time. At last I went over to reassure him, hoping I could convince him that we were just waiting for all "his" people to arrive.

"Hey, Tim," I said. "Where's that guy from Reuters? And I haven't seen Mike Mills yet . . ."

Findley gestured out into the Bay, not far from where I had been looking, to where a motorized skiff bobbed in the water, half way out to Alcatraz. "That's them. They're waiting for you," and he shot me a quizzical, skeptical look.

It had all the signs of a major public relations disaster in progress. The media was there, some of them even waiting in a boat of their own. The Indians were there, I counted at least seventy. Where were my boats?

Richard looked husky and fit, and I loaned him a beaded headband to add some dash to his handsomely thick dark hair. He definitely had the appearance of a Mohawk who might, indeed, have earned his muscles in high steel, but he had a cast in his eye for me that suggested some doubt.

"Okay," I said to him. "Here, take the Proclamation and get on one of those piers and read it. Keep reading it. I gotta get us ready."

This was the moment, I think, that established Richard in what the media called his "Victor Mature" image, the moment he took leadership of this Indian resurgence. He stood on the pier post (a high shot for the cameras) with the bright day and the Bay behind him, and began to read the Proclamation.

To the Great White Father and All His People:
We, the Native Americans, reclaim the land known as Alcatraz Island in the name of all American Indians by right of discovery.[4]

It was a pretty long proclamation. (Its full text appears in this appendix of this book.) The point just then, though, was that it would take Richard a fair amount of time to get through it all.

There was a public phone a few yards away. I had to get a dime from Bobbie to make the call. "No," "Jerry's" told me, "they had no boats available, none at all." I felt like arguing, like accusing somebody of the double-cross. But from the phone booth I noticed something I hadn't seen before.

There, rocking very gently in the quiet morning swells was an ornately outfitted vessel—a ship, actually, masted and rigged just like something that must have brought the pilgrims to shore. Standing on her at the top of the gangplank in what seemed a posture that was just bored and idle enough to be watching what was going on with the crowd of Indians was a guy who apparently was outfitted in his own traditional regalia. He had a white shirt with billowy sleeves and a lacy sort of tie. His dark pants were held up by a hugely oversized belt, and I looked hard to be sure that, yes, that was a sword he had on his side.

Kismet, I think they call it. Me in my quill roach and flower-beaded yoke dashing up the gangplank in my moccasins to the outstretched hand of this bloused and booted buccaneer, his smile reaching all the way from sideburn to sideburn.

"Yeah? Really?" Capt. Ronald Craig (the Count of Monte Cristo, as he called himself) said with growing interest. "You guys just want to go around the island for the news people?"

Craig, just thirty-seven himself, and his replicated 136-foot clipper barque the *Monte Cristo* had been at the wharf for a couple of weeks or more, picking up charter tours to pay their way as they headed down the

Pacific coast. Only the month before, Craig said, they had gotten publicity and even a plaque from the Navy for staging a blank cannon "attack" on the old battleship *New Jersey* docked in Seattle.

I listened eagerly, hearing and nodding faster than he could talk. Richard, I could see from the ship, was already passing the Proclamation on to someone else to read from. "Could we, I mean, wow, the publicity . . ."

"Well, okay, it's a slow Sunday anyway," Craig agreed. "But no more than fifty on board, okay? And we'll only go around a couple of times."

I was already halfway down the gangplank.

They didn't call me "Fortunate Eagle" in those days. That name would come later. But call it what you want, the day, and maybe the whole movement itself, was saved because I had the luck and the outright brass to do one of those kinds of things that even my wife sometimes called embarrassing. Think about it, though. Could a more plainly dressed or cautiously polite character have done it?

Waving more Indians aboard and counting them along with Captain Craig, I noticed Findley standing down there on the dock gazing up with that suspicious look again. He caught my eye and shrugged his hands up in a gesture meaning, "What's this?" I grinned back and copied his gesture.

It should have always been hard to miss Joe Bill, but I think this was the first time I really took notice of the happy-go-lucky Inuit who climbed aboard with the rest, his flat-topped reservation hat that shaded his long hair and his colorful knit poncho like a signature of his reputation. He beamed at me and gave me a quick shake of a half-closed fist.

Maybe I can be too flamboyant for some at times, but taking to sea it's hard to outdo someone like the Count of Monte Cristo. Craig ordered a couple of loud cannon bursts as we backed our way out, just to signal the start of the mission. Then, flying the maple leaf flag of his Canadian registry, we set off on what was certainly one of the strangest acts of even mock war ever to have occurred in an American harbor. I think it was on the second pass, after we had fired the cannon again and come around in a tighter circle only about a hundred yards off the island, that the same thought must have occurred to both of us at once.

"Say," he asked me with a little crinkle of worry in his voice, "nobody's going to jump off or anything?"

"Oh, nooo," I said, shaking my quilled head and trying to estimate if any of them really could swim that far.

Richard's own reputation was on the line about this, I think. Despite what La Nada said later, our original plan had not been merely to circle around the island in some symbolic display. We had meant to use those five boats to land there, and some of us had brought along food and blankets for a possible long stay. Richard had gathered his supporters with the promise of some sort of landing and occupation. It couldn't just stop with a morning sail and a few pictures.

To Craig's loudly expressed horror at the sight, I think Richard was the first one off the bow.

"NO! No more!" Craig tried to order, uncertain yet of whether to turn away or try a rescue. "Tell them not to jump! Tell them no more of that!"

"Don't jump! Don't jump!" I dutifully shouted, but there were two more loud splashes and accompanying cheers. Curiously, the do-anything young Inuit, Joe Bill, only watched, although I could see him start to strip off his poncho and his shirt as Craig, crossing more on the eastward lee side of the island, began shouting orders to "come about."

"What the hell are they doing?" the captain demanded of me as he watched the swimmers arm-splashing away from his ship in legendarily dangerous water.

"Well, they want to reclaim Alcatraz for Indian people, they . . ."

"Re-CLAIM? Re-CLAIM!" he yelled back. "Can't you see it's like an act of war? Can't you see my flag?" He shoved his own bullhorn in my hand. "Tell them! No MORE!"

"No more jumping!" I ordered, impressed with the volume of the electronic gadget.

Joe Bill, a good deal more sea-wise than the other young men from inland reservations, had calculated and planned his nicely arched dive to match the current as closely as possible. He went over (with a groan from Captain Craig) and was actually the first to reach the island. We could see him from the *Monte Cristo* as he climbed up the rocks and waved his arms in triumph. Even Captain Craig, I think, was cheering along with the rest of us.

Richard's fate had very nearly ended with more tragic results. Coughing and retching, he was hauled aboard the skiff on which Findley had joined other photo teams filming the show. They were headed on to rescue another of the floundering swimmers when Richard jumped off again, daring fate a second time, but happily this time was carried by the current onto the island's rocky shore.

We had heard that the new caretaker on the island, a twenty-year prison veteran named John Hart, kept a large vicious dog to discourage intruders. When Richard made it to shore and linked up with another of the successful swimmers, Ross Harden, they found Joe Bill and that irrepressible smile of his sitting on the rocks with the dog behind him, wagging its tail.

It didn't last long, of course, not even as long as the Sioux stand had in 1964. Captain Craig, more concerned with what the Coast Guard vessels may have been watching than spending time being angry with us, took us quickly back to the wharf. On the island it hadn't taken long for Hart and his helpers to find the three Indians. He met them with another of those memorable one-liners I mentioned before.

"Get the hell off this island," he commanded.

■

The trouble with the future these days is that it lacks imagination. Not true then, not in the ending days of the sixties. Imagination, ideas, those were what was real then, not like now when you need technical training for them.

Richard and the other swimmers were brought off the island by the Coast Guard, receiving no real criminal charges except a stern warning. Those of us waiting chipped in for a sort of celebratory lunch. We had not altogether failed. At the very least it had been a grand show, maybe even better than what we had promised the media. The Proclamation, read at least twice on the dock, would be used to carry the visual message of the swimmers themselves. As we reassembled in scattered groups at the temporary headquarters of the San Francisco Indian Center, we could at least say we had drawn attention to the center's cause, and to our cause in general.

But we still didn't have Alcatraz, and maybe the government thought we had shot our full wad in a grandiose clipper ship attempt to get it. I don't cuss. It's just something a lot of us older Indians regard as being very offensive and degrading. But I was still thinking, "What the hell happened to my boats!?" A lot later on somebody told me that at least one of those boats had shown up at the dock before I got there and that the captain had been convinced by a mysterious woman that he and the others would be risking their livelihoods by taking Indians out for a pointless landing. Supposedly it was an Indian woman, but I've never known for sure if that story was true.

Richard and the other young people were inspired and exhausted enough by the *Monte Cristo* experience to not lay blame on me or anybody. The question was, How to get to the island? We figured the government wouldn't be expecting another attempt, certainly not another on the same day. One more time, as news was spreading from the radio stations about the afternoon's flamboyant "assault," I started calling the boat people I knew on Fisherman's Wharf.

The *New Vera II* was one of those long-railed fishing boats working the trade for sport salmon charters. Her captain told me he had seen parts of the great adventure earlier in the day. If we really wanted to go to Alcatraz, he said, he'd take us, for a price.

Fourteen gets to be an important number in some recollections of all this. La Nada, for example, has said that there was an attempt to land on the island on October 14, only four days after the Indian Center burned. Others have said it was November 14, seven days before a more important event. Actually the number was somewhere around twenty when we counted all the Indians, including Earl Livermore, La Nada, the ever-ready Joe Bill, and me, who met the *New Vera II* just after twilight that same day of November 9. Richard was not among the group. He had insisted on going home to his student housing for a change of clothes and to pack a sleeping bag and some food that we all agreed would be needed. We waited for him at the crowded dock in Fisherman's Wharf for as long as the impatient skipper would allow. The captain had already cast off one line and was about to set out when Richard came running down from the pier.

The kind of thing I think that gets boat captains nervous is those unpredictable, last-minute changes. Earl had paid in advance for the boat, and he and I had done our best to assure the captain that after all the day's attentions we could expect nothing more than a quiet, unheralded visit to the uncoveted island. But the skipper could see the sleeping bags and the loads of food for such a short evening's venture. Richard, loudly announcing himself with a leap onto the deck, may have been the captain's last clue.

We did get out to the water barge that rode against the concrete loading dock of the old prison. Even in the dark, being coldly swept by the passing lighthouse beacon, the old signs in large red letters warning mariners off from the federal property were still readable. A boat owner could lose his vessel for this, he could wind up in jail. But we had paid for the *New Vera II* to take us at least that close, and as the fishing boat bumped up against the old tires draped along the hull of the barge somebody, maybe it was Richard, threw up a line and leaped behind it to tie our hired landing craft to a temporary mooring.

The young people started scrambling off, carrying what they could in one arm, reaching behind to help others up and across. The captain grew increasingly alarmed at this. "Ah, damn it. Damn it," I heard him muttering. Suddenly, but fairly smoothly, he reversed engines and backed away from the barge. The line snapped with a pop, and those of us still waiting to jump from the bow fell back into the boat.

Fourteen, however, had made it ashore, completely unnoticed by the caretakers who thought their day's work had been done.

Back again on the wharf I called Findley, whose deadline for the final Monday morning edition was still at least a couple of hours away.

Findley called John Hart at the phone number the press had for Alcatraz emergencies.

"What about the Indians out there?" the reporter asked.

"What Indians?" Hart hotly replied. "There aren't any more Indians!"

9

The Landing, November 9, 1969

IN THE LONG, ADVENTUROUS NIGHT that followed, La Nada discovered the distinction across a line that was to grow deeper and deeper between intention and ambition in the Alcatraz occupation.

"On the island, you can hide just about anywhere, and no one can find you," she remembered. "And they would be so close sometimes, they'd be coming by so close, and it was almost like someone would be tickling you and you'd be trying to keep back your laughter because you didn't want to give yourself away. We felt like such kids."[1]

Despite his denials, caretaker John Hart had to take the press inquiries seriously. Somehow Indians must have come aboard the island without being seen. He began a long, cautious search with a flashlight, uncertain and a little nervous about what he might find. Hart was trained and experienced in dealing with convicts whose desperate desire was to get off the hell off the Rock. There was nothing to tell him what to expect from strangely persistent Indians who wanted to stay on it. Carefully, he cast his beam along the shoreline and over the docks, losing it in the complicated and eerie shadows. But he had it backwards. Instinctively he was looking where a guard might look for a prisoner hiding and cringing at the prospect of still having to cross the treacherous Bay.

As the night went on he alerted the Coast Guard, which sent out a small cutter that cruised around close to shore, playing its big searchlight against the rocks and the steep hillsides shielded from Hart's small beam.

But the fourteen Indians had long since dodged past the dock, running close together through the short ink-dark tunnel that led them up the slippery exposed cobblestones toward the main cell block and the empty warden's residence that dominated the highest points on the island. Whispering amongst themselves as they huddled in the gloom of the open building, they agreed to split up into groups of threes. Even if one group were found, it would not lead to the others. They divided the food, a preposterous survival ration of sourdough bread and random sandwiches that was all they had had time to assemble hastily. And then, knowing they were like children who'd slipped away for their first gigglingly scary look at the night, they began to explore.

Hart's dog was of no real use, but something in the excitement of the animal as it dashed about the island seemed to confirm his growing suspicion. Somebody had told the reporters about the Indians. There had to be some truth to the story. Still, it was useless and maybe risky to carry on that search in the dark. Hart notified his superiors that at first light he would need more help to conduct a thorough search.

Findley and other reporters needed more convincing, too. Calling me back after checks with the island, they made it clear they did not intend to be "had" with a false report. The *Chronicle* would go with the story that morning, but if no proof appeared by the next day, our credibility with the media was finished for good. With those early editions of the morning paper all the media was alerted. Calls to the island, to the Coast Guard, to the U.S. attorney's office, and to federal marshals soon built up a cadre of reporters demanding to see for themselves what the government intended to do about "invading" Indians.[2]

The press came out that morning in an armada of their own, bigger than anything we could have hoped to assemble. Most of the reporters were crowded aboard a Coast Guard vessel along with the designated official leader of the search, General Services Administrator Tom Hannon. Hannon was basically a landlord and real estate agent for the federal government. It was not normally in his job description to deal with anything more than an occasional vagrant or, lately, with some loose hippies who might try to take up residence in an old warehouse or a leftover barracks somewhere. But it didn't make sense to U.S. Attorney Cecil Poole to approach the problem as if it were some kind of resumption of the old Indian wars. Especially because the press was in tow, he stressed a calm, unarmed search that would end peacefully in a little more media exposure for what he still saw as a hopeless Indian cause. In any case, Poole knew his own position would soon be occupied by a Nixon appointee.

By daylight the real condition of Alcatraz and the old federal prison were even more apparent. Few if any of the reporters had been to the island since at least 1964, and a couple of the senior press people who remembered it from the time it was an active prison were amazed at how much it had deteriorated since then. Snarling, prickly vines of blackberries tangled themselves in and about the old concrete railings and steps, which in many places were cracked and broken from the weather, revealing the rusted iron skeletons of reinforcing bars. The catwalks along the outside of the cell block and other buildings appeared in places to be just dangling from thin red shreds of oxidized bolts and braces. It seemed that nothing had been touched since that last convict left in 1963, leaving all the towers and steps and buildings open to the damp fog that smothered it and ate away at the abandoned fortress.

All of that attracted the reporters' attention at least as much as the touring search for Indians did. Alcatraz, even as it still does today, held a fascination of its own as if, surely, ghosts might be there among the slowly crumbling ruins.

"We could see them," La Nada remembered. "The press and all those feds, and they were looking for us, but we were still hiding out, and nobody could be found."[3]

Findley, lagging behind from what he always disparaged as "the pack" of media in such cases, stopped near the stone retaining wall beneath the cell block and leaned back to light a cigarette.

"Hey, Tim," came a scratchy voice from behind him.

"Aww, JEE-sus, Richard," Findley said, startled and stumbling back onto the cobble-paved road. "You scared the hell out of me!"

It had not been loud enough for the others to hear. They were making their way past the warden's house through the flat little courtyard at the top of the hill that led into the cell block. Poking his head through a small window the reporter had not even noticed before, Richard grinned in triumph.

"Who are those guys?" he said.

"Feds, of course. I dunno, some guy from GSA who wants to talk to you."[4]

"Okay. Tell 'em to come down here."

La Nada, later on at least, regarded Richard's response as a betrayal.

"And then the press arrived, and Richard gets up and declares himself the leader and gives us all up," she remembered. "We were a little upset about that, why he did that, and we cussed him out about it later."[5]

Richard, however, had seized his own time and, indirectly at least, his own conditions for what inevitably would have had to be a surrender, whether or not, as La Nada incorrectly believed, there were more Indians on the mainland planning to reinforce the fourteen occupiers. Alone among them Richard felt he had a personal standing with the newspeople. It would not always be such an advantage as it was that morning.

If you really must have a landlord and you can't pay your rent, Tom Hannon might have been a good model for an understanding eviction. Hannon, tall and somewhat disproportional in his facial features, quietly stood in front of his small force, waiting as Richard gradually lured the others out of hiding. To the patient GSA man Richard insisted on reading the Proclamation, defiantly calculating his words for the listening press. Hannon tried to begin with an explanation that it was not his decision to make, but that the safety of anyone on the island, whatever their cause, could not be assured by the government. "It's a dangerous, hopelessly unsuitable place," he tried to explain, and the media listened to that too, comparing notes to what had been said in the Proclamation.

"Well, if you're ready to leave now, I can offer you a ride," Hannon concluded, gesturing to his own little flotilla of Coast Guard vessels.

Richard glanced around, seeming to satisfy himself that it would be on his terms.

"Let's go," he said, not waiting for Hannon as he stepped off toward the dock.

■

Our job, that of Earl Livermore and me especially, was to continue fending off the calls that began coming in to the Indian Center from all over California, and then from all over the country as the story and film of the previous day's *Monte Cristo* event was spread and enlivened by verified accounts of a later landing. It had captured some imagination in the general media, even more so because in those still relatively early days of television coverage the film of Richard with the Proclamation and then the bizarre sail around the Bay was spreading all over the country.

But if we had the excitement of handling the media, we also had the more tricky and serious task of lining up whatever support might be necessary after the government made its move. We didn't know if everybody might be arrested, jailed, and in need of bail, or if there might even be a fight out there. Up to then we had not been consulting with lawyers on any basis other than knowing who among us could make the right calls if and when the time came.

That night we invited an attorney, R. Courbin Houchins of the "movement"-aligned firm of Hodge, Houchins and Zweig, to sit in on our discussions about what we were planning next. I should note here that Richard Hodge of that firm had worked on notorious Black Panther cases, among others, and was destined himself to become a judge, but in those early days we were just looking for a little advice on what we might expect from federal authorities. Houchins provided it with some realistic observations in a letter he sent on November 13: "There are also some serious charges which in all probability would not be made by the United States Attorney, but of which I should apprise you," he wrote. "It is a capital crime to levy war against the United States; it is a felony to incite, start, assist, give aid or comfort to, or engage in a rebellion or insurrection; it is a felony to conspire to seize, take or possess any federal property."[6]

On the other hand Houchins saw things from another perspective, too, especially "the fact that it is also a felony to retain the property of any tribe subject to federal law regulating Indian affairs, knowing the same to have been stolen, with intent to convert it to the use of someone other than the rightful owner. We may wish to press charges!" the lawyer suggested.

For the time being, though, Hannon was as good as his word. Our fourteen "scouts" were returned to the mainland and simply released. I don't think the feds even took names.

La Nada may have been furious at Richard for giving them up so easily and for taking the leadership role without any discussion, but at the Indian Center we had a victorious, proudly excited reunion. It actually could not have gone better if our original plans had worked. If those five boats I was promised had shown up, we might have made the surprise landing we hoped for and gotten into whatever symbolic confrontation we would encounter with Hart and his caretakers. It could have lasted a few hours on a Sunday and probably have ended in a way similar to what happened in 1964. There's no Indian word for "serendipity" that I know about, so I think maybe something bigger than coincidence provided us with the sure spectacle of Captain Craig and his clipper barque. And if the importance of that event was possible only because of my own brash and costumed rush on Craig, then time would show that it was also significant that I had turned over to Richard my planned duty of reading the Proclamation.

All over the country now, in a way we could not have planned or managed, two images of Indians merged in a unique way. One was that of a group of tribal outfits coming back from the past and seeming to "commandeer" a replicated piece of European history. The other, perhaps even more tempting to the imagination, was the strikingly photogenic young Mohawk whose reading of the Proclamation was followed up by more than just a media bluff. There was something quite colorful but strangely serious happening on the West Coast.

Richard was carried away by it. He was an instant celebrity—handsome, articulate, and incredibly daring. Hollywood stuff, and it wasn't missed by the critically opportunistic eyes in Los Angeles.

I can't be sure from my memory if Mary Lou Justice was among the three women (which included La Nada) who made that first landing. But Mary Lou was always the stabilizing, detail-conscious member of Richard and Al's team from San Francisco State. Certainly she was as dedicated and often as intense as La Nada, but less impatient. Mary Lou didn't seem to mind accepting a role behind the scenes, out of the media focus, where she could go on with the demanding work of assembling all the logistics.

As much as it was La Nada who carried the message back to Berkeley, I'm pretty sure it was Mary Lou who made the important contacts with people at UCLA and Southern Cal. Richard made the speeches as a recognized news celebrity, but Mary Lou took care of all the details.

From at least November 9 on there was never any doubt among us that there would have to be another landing, done in greater numbers and with far more advance planning. We knew everything we needed to know, except whether the government would now be preparing for such an attempt. The Christmas season was the most logical target date. The weather in the Bay Area at that time could still be expected to be relatively calm, and the authorities would be distracted by the holidays. Most important, the students would be on extended break from the campuses, giving us a reliable force for something more impressive.

But there were problems with that too. The publicity was going strong all over the country, stronger than we could have hoped. There was an enthusiasm building that was like trying to hold back racing thoroughbreds at the starting gate. We knew that if we didn't take advantage of that energy in a timely way, it might merely fade out into more discussions.

Self-proclaimed militants like Lehman Brightman and even some of the other Sioux in the East Bay still regarded it as just posturing for the media, clownish and ultimately insignificant. But the core of students and young people from the Little Res, along with those of us willing to accept a role as elder planners and organizers, were more determined than ever. If Christmas was too long to wait, then we only had less than two weeks to pull it off during the Thanksgiving holiday.

The first National Conference on Indian Education was set for that time to be held in Minneapolis. I saw it as a perfect opportunity for me as a delegate to the conference to draw in with a dramatic announcement even broader support among the intellectuals and academics. It would be the perfect time, that is, if Richard and the other students could assemble the essential details.

Findley also says he still can't be sure if the pretty young woman who arrived first that evening more than a week later to wait with him for Richard was Mary Lou Justice, but it seems almost certain that it had to have been. Richard was a little late, but the reporter was by now used to that. He chatted with the young woman while they waited in the *Chronicle*'s hangout, Hanno's-in-the-Alley, a little corner bar directly behind the double buildings shared by both the morning and evening papers in San Francisco.

Hanno's was more than just a bar. It had red formica tables and plastic cushions on the seats, but every hour it was open, from 6:00 A.M. to 2:00 A.M., Hanno's was likely to be the center of the best journalistic secrets in town, told among what were in those days some of the most vibrant writers the West Coast had to offer.

Richard was instantly recognized when he finally did come in, although the other reporters there at the time lost none of their own jaded cynicism by acknowledging it with more than a raised eyebrow.

Spilling over with his usual exuberance, Richard explained the contacts he had made at San Jose State and the overwhelming acceptance he had found at UCLA. There was nothing to stop them, he told Findley, and the young woman seemed quietly to agree. Findley, cursed all his life by such problems, was trying to figure out in his head how he might put all the beers he was buying on his expense report. He was putting them away at least as fast as Richard was, and though that wasn't really the problem, Richard was leading up to something by laying out all the elaborate arrangements already in motion.

"There's one thing," he finally confided. "We still don't know where to find the boats for it."

Findley was wary of being drawn too far into this evident conspiracy. There were serious professional risks at stake, even if he was known to be a little reckless at observing the rules. They talked for more than an hour, and Richard never mentioned that he had left Annie and the kids waiting for him outside in their car.

Suddenly Annie burst through the swinging doors, obviously steaming from Richard's long absence, and then was at the point of eruption when she spotted him sitting with the reporter and another young Indian woman.

Richard calmed her down. The waitress brought over another drink to add to the clutter of beer bottles on the little table. Annie sat across from the young woman, glaring from her to Richard, obviously worried about the kids still sitting in the car. Richard, though, kept talking. Just a little too long.

Without warning Annie grabbed one of the beer bottles by the neck and flung it full force across the table, right at the eye of the other young woman.

Maybe she wasn't Mary Lou Justice, but from that point on no one remembers her carrying on with what had been her important role in creating Indian Alcatraz.

10

The Invasion, November 20, 1969

As MUCH AS THE MEDIA WANTED, and for their purposes *needed*, to present Richard in the starring role as the leader of the Alcatraz invasion and occupation, it was not quite that simple. With much the same storied necessity that still presents Sitting Bull and Crazy Horse as having command of the battles at the Little Big Horn, the legends about Richard evolved in many ways from the "image" that was beyond even his control.

There is no doubt that once he felt sure of himself, Richard presented an authentic charisma that drew others to him. But the young Mohawk was never quite in charge of all the converging events any more than I was, or Earl Livermore was, or La Nada was. The idea seemed almost to take charge of itself, like static in the air.

Richard's visit to UCLA came at another of those moments when energy was colliding into focus. Ed Castillo had only that year been hired as a graduate student instructor in UCLA's own emerging Native American Studies program. Castillo's story is similar to what was experienced by many members of California tribes who found themselves in the confusing limbo of nonexistence after the rush to terminate the state's reservations and rancherias in the 1950s. He is a Cahuilla-Luiseño raised on his rancheria outside San Jacinto. As a teenager and later as a student at the University of California at Riverside, however, Ed was taken by his teachers and even fellow students to be Hispanic. Not until he was a senior writing his thesis on Indians at Mission San Diego did he proclaim his own tribal roots. Up to then, he recalls, no one had asked.

At UCLA, as at Native American Studies programs all across the West, students were drawn by their own interest and by their instructors to reexamine first how the past had been stolen from their tribal identities. Anthropologists had collected the culture and the customs and attempted to preserve them like specimens. Old Indians were even removed from their graves and put on display in museums.

Ed Castillo and his students were on the verge of turning that around by digging up the grave of an old white Indian fighter in a military cemetery that neighbored the campus. Just before the specimen-producing demonstration could be carried out with its intended shock value, Richard showed up with the idea for Alcatraz.

"He was a good-looking man, powerful and articulate," Castillo remembered. "It was eloquent the way he put the proposal to us. It sounded like a good idea, something new."[1] The reaction had been the same at Berkeley, and at San Jose State and, of course, in San Francisco and the Little Res where all the energy began aiming. It was part Richard, part Al Miller and Mary Lou Justice and La Nada Means, but it was also part media, and in ways beyond any of their influence, it was partly the times. There was a certain sanction for dissent in those days, almost as if the limits had to be tested, as if it was not just a right of youth but even an obligation of young people living in those times to declare their own liberated way. Perhaps no other students reacted with more enthusiasm than mine and E. E. Papke's at San Quentin Prison. Though they couldn't be there to participate, there was unanimous agreement that it was a fine idea.

At "Kayo" Hallinan's massive New Mobilization March Against the War on November 15, at least a quarter of a million people had gathered in Golden Gate Park. They heard the classic free concert by the Mamas and the Papas, Jefferson Airplane, and others. They cheered with understanding of the metaphor when Black Panther chief of staff David Hilliard said somebody ought to "kill" Richard Nixon. The undercover agents in the crowd were far less appreciative of the rhetoric.

It was events such as those that drew federal officials to develop a case against Hilliard and expand their own network of agents within the antiwar movement that played some part in diverting law enforcement attention away from the likelihood of any more trouble with Indians on Alcatraz. As the recruitment and planning went on we kept the secret as best we could, but we knew as word spread to Los Angeles and even further that it would be impossible to maintain internal security for long.

Ed Castillo flew up on his own credit card. His students, at least a third of his class, took a more perilously traceable route by checking out three UCLA-owned station wagons for a "field trip" they did not quite reveal was headed for San Francisco. Castillo remembers everybody feeling "really paranoid" by the time they arrived in the midst of another meeting at the temporary Indian Center on Mission Street: "There was this rancorous meeting going on, debating the merits of going to the island immediately or putting off the occupation. I recall walking in with a member of my tribe, a young woman named Sue Kitchen, and as we walked by the door, a guy who appeared to be a non-Indian—a guy with long blonde hair, kind of a biker type—stood up and said 'I think the police are on to you and I don't think you should be going.' And somebody walked up beside him and just blindsided him, just hit him a good one. Knocked him out cold."

■

Designated leader or media creation, actually in command or not, it was that kind of spirit Richard would have to direct or lose control of altogether. Only one major problem really stood in his way: there were still no boats.

"Look, Tim, you guys must know somebody," he appealed to the reporter. It had only been a day or two since their conversation at the bar was interrupted by a young woman's visit to the emergency room. "Just give me some names," Richard argued. "We'll take it from there."

The ultimate choice for Findley wasn't just in whether to get further involved with the obvious momentum for an Indian Alcatraz, but whether he could even do it without exposing himself and his paper. I was on my way to Minneapolis, carrying a whole ream of proclamations prepared by Dorothy Miller and ready to be distributed the minute I got word of our success. This time boats were Richard's problem.

The reporter told Richard he'd call him back that afternoon. There was one possibility Findley knew we had overlooked. At that Halloween party, among the reporters and the politicians and the obvious activists, there were also at least one or two representatives of the "Sausalito Navy." Findley even remembered them joking in the kitchen that night about painting some dinghies to look like canoes.

The "Navy" was based and berthed generally in a rebellious and free-spirited maze of rag-tag and roughly assembled planks and piers that connected imaginatively homemade houseboats, patched-up sailing vessels, and vintage craft of wildly assorted description together in Richardson Bay, a steep, snooty look down from the rich homes on the Sausalito hillsides.

It was partly this disparity between the unaffordable opulence of the hill dwellers—some of them even rock stars like Janis Joplin—and the fifteen-buck-a-bag survival skills of water-borne hippies in the Bay that made the "Navy" a unique, almost piratical group in themselves. Findley thought he only knew one of them, former *Chronicle* reporter Brooks Townes, well enough to ask, but Brooks reminded him that Peter Bowen owned the best motorsailer of the lot.

Bowen was the sort of self-made character that the sixties were all about. He had a much-prized handlebar mustache that could not conceal his frequent grins and the cackle of laughter he found at almost anything taking itself too seriously. Not that Bowen didn't tend to business. He ran a small walkup scrimshaw shop along the pricey Sausalito shopping street and was himself a skilled carver in ivory. But that was the gravy. His real living came as the bartender, manager and, as some assumed, eventual owner of the No Name Bar, the most eclectically exclusive hangout north of the Golden Gate. Writers, artists, reporters, rising young lawyers, and denizens of the waterfront mingled there nightly, sometimes well beyond closing hour.

"Yeah?" Bowen cackled. "They're gonna do it, huh?" He let it sink in for a long, conspiratorial moment, then said, "Let me check with some people."

Findley was distancing himself from making the news by being certain that the Indians themselves could call Peter. But the *Chronicle* reporter was also making sure he would be in on it himself. It is telling of how the organization was evolving that Bowen remembers getting the call at the agreed-upon time that evening not from Richard Oakes, but from Al Miller.

Richard to Tim to Brooks to Peter to Al and back to Richard. That was the path of strategic planning and, if you like, conspiracy for what surely was the strangest and most originally assembled invasion of United States territory in history. It might also have been the most successful one.

■

All these many years later some people persist in the belief that the pre-dawn invasion on November 20 was launched, at least in part, from the Berkeley marina. Things get mixed up in memories sometimes, and there's no doubt that some adventures still ahead began from the East Bay. But not that night, certainly not with the official and public notice implied by one absurd account presented in the U.S. Park Service's authorized version sold today on the island. Maybe one reason later historians who weren't there so often get it wrong is because what really happened is almost too unlikely to believe.

The carloads of Indians began arriving after 1:00 A.M., taking the first exit north of the Golden Gate Bridge that led them down the gently curving two-lane road, past the fashionably upscale homes on the hillsides and the poshly hip bars and restaurants like the Kingston Trio's Trident (built out into the calm Bay with its stunning views of the city). Around one last left-turning corner they came into the Sausalito business district, its long row of exclusively priced shops and amber-lit bars standing shoulder-to-shoulder on one side of the street. They would have to look carefully to spot one place that called itself the No Name. Only a discreetly illuminated shingle hung outside its entrance, and the windows gave it away no more than all the other fern-shaded fronts in all the other trendy establishments. It was a Wednesday night into Thursday morning, generally a drowsy, peaceful time along the Sausalito waterfront after about 11:00 P.M. It was mostly locals who were still in the bars after that time, and the town's small police force was accustomed to waiting for the 2:00 A.M. closing hour before paying really close attention to the dimly lit sidewalks and the small public parking lot sheltered by well-established trees between the shopping front and the yacht harbor. At most the cops could expect to stop a couple of drunk drivers, or maybe break up a brief scuffle. Sausalito, especially in the wee hours of a Thursday, didn't see much trouble from the people who could afford to be there.

Ed Castillo and his students at first had been led to believe that they would meet Richard and the others somewhere in Berkeley. When he received the call directing them to Sausalito, he was not even quite sure where Sausalito was. They drove across the Bay Bridge into San Francisco, stopping at Warren's to double-check the directions. No one was expected to find the No Name itself. Instead they were told to find a not-too-obvious parking space and begin gathering around the harbor.

Findley perched on a barstool near the front of the place, next to *Chronicle* photographer Vince Maggiora, another Sausalito resident. Quietly the reporter kept an eye out the No Name's high window, trying to count the figures he saw moving across the street under back-bending bundles they carried with them toward the waterfront. He swallowed a beer and glanced again at Peter. The No Name's popular manager had turned his usual place behind the bar over to one of his employees and sat instead at a small corner table near the back of the place where it opened into a shaded courtyard. Sitting with him were Brooks and five others with obvious attachments to the style of seafarers. The reporter knew that the handful of patrons still at the bar by this time would hold on to their glasses until the last minute. Again Findley looked out the window. There were more shadows headed in an uncertain path toward the needles of masts they could barely make out in the harbor. The police had noticed, too. Findley saw their white patrol car cruise slowly by and then make the loop around the little landscaped plaza before going into the parking lot and out again in a sort of suspicious lazy eight, not quite certain of what they were seeing. It would be another couple of days before the Sausalito officers determined that the state-owned license plates on at least two of the over-parked cars belonged to UCLA.

Peter's arrangements had been that only one of the Indians, probably Al

Miller, would come into the bar and let him know when the rest were ready. To the startled surprise of the lingering bar mavens and to quick shuffling by Peter and his cohorts, however, at least half a dozen Indians, including Al and Richard, suddenly appeared in the doorway. The trick was to get them seated and served like normal and begin filtering them back out before the puzzled cops themselves showed up. Which, in fact, they did, making a casual-looking entrance with their thumbs in their belts and recognizing Peter right away when he stepped up to greet them. Nope, no problem, he assured the gendarmes. Just one of those nights. The cops nodded with their usual doubtful agreement before heading back on their way; Findley said it felt like letting the air out of a balloon.

Trusting his bartender with the night's final duties, Peter led the last small group of Indians seated at his tables out across the quiet street and down to the yacht harbor. Located a bit south of where the most outlandish and yet remarkably still-floating houseboats held a sort of water-squatters enclave, the Sausalito yacht harbor was a mix of the semi-serious and surreal. There were plenty of finely outfitted day sailers of fiberglass that traced their financial lineage up the hillside, a few even more opulently prepared craft resting for a time from serious ocean voyages, and a scattering of the average rent-a-boats. It was a fairly dignified, country-club set of a yacht harbor, with the noticeable exception of the raucously piratical mix of the Sausalito Navy. Most of the Indians were standing in a long line on a tilting and unsure platform of the floating pier that led between the slips. Peter could see immediately that there were more of them than he had expected. "Oh, geez," he muttered. There were more than he had time to find life jackets for. More, in fact, than the three boats he had lined up, including his own *Seaweed*, could possibly accommodate in one trip.

Brooks, meanwhile, had noticed something even more disturbing. "I think they've got the Rock lit up like a Christmas tree," he said in an awed, unconscious whisper. He pointed to a spot out past the Spinnaker Restaurant where there was just enough of a gap to get a look from Richardson Bay south across the inky water into greater San Francisco Bay itself. Just about where Alcatraz should have been a mere silhouette beneath a lighthouse, there did indeed appear to be a very brightly illuminated and glittering object as large as an imaginary island. "Can't be," Peter said, squinting hard at the thing. "It's not moving," said Brooks. They looked again, trying to judge impossible distances in the dark.

Brooks at last volunteered to make use of a motorized skiff. He hummed off on his mission to reconnoiter the strange light while the rest of them waited, tilting and swaying on the floating pier. Brooks was gone for the best part of a tense half hour before returning in a motor-washed curl at the dock.

"S'okay," he gasped. "It's just a sand dredge well to this side of the island. The Rock is dark as hell."

Peter, meanwhile, was trying to make some count and sort out how it could be done to get the invasion under way before daylight. There were too many. Some of the Indians, he said, would have to wait for a second trip, and the haggling over who that would be took up still more time.

Thirty-six, including the two *Chronicle* staffers, finally boarded the *Seaweed*. She was, and is, a very special wooden motorsailer of about thirty-two feet of a vintage you might describe as Humphrey Bogart. Peter actually lived on board in a sort of tended hard-bunk splendor lightly decorated with his own art work. A second group of twenty or more went aboard Bob Teft's even more classically varnished wood-hulled thirty-eight-foot Chris Craft cabin cruiser, the *Odin II*, and the last of the first wave went with Mary Crowley in her almost-restored thirty-foot Czechoslovakian "double-ender" sailboat, also wood-hulled during a time of greater craftsmanship. This was the total invasion fleet.

As they began pulling out of the harbor with Peter taking the lead, Mary was having trouble with the engine on her boat. The *Seaweed* was out and Teft's *Odin* was casting off, but the motor on Mary's boat still wouldn't start. Determined not to be left behind on this adventure, Mary began unfurling her sails. It requires some remarkable daring and a good deal of skill to rely solely on the wind during the best of moonlit evenings on the Bay, let alone in the darkest part of a tense mid-November night before dawn, but Mary was not about to be left behind, even if none of her passengers knew the risk.

Mary looked to be in a confident state of early adulthood, certainly old enough and experienced enough to be hanging out with her fellow Sausalito sailors at the No Name. She was a graduate of Loyola University in Chicago, a yacht handler of some local renown, and that seemed impressive for one bright young woman of what everyone assumed was twenty-three or twenty-four or so. Actually, she was just eighteen.

Out on the Bay Peter was troubling himself over how little his own hasty invasion plans were working out. There were more Indians on board than he had intended, more than he had life jackets for, and his plan to keep them below decks to avoid being seen was hopeless. He didn't know it, but even his firmest rule about "no children" had already been violated by La Nada, who was smuggling on her two-year-old son, Deynon. Peter's memory is of stepping into the wheelhouse on the way out and being startled by a squeal from beneath a blanket. Twelve-year-old Yvonne Oakes was on board as well. Too late to do more than grumble, he put the *Seaweed* on course for the Bay.

La Nada and her son, Deynon, with other occupiers, below deck on Peter Bowen's boat *Seaweed,* November 20, 1969. Photograph by Vincent Maggiora, courtesy of *San Francisco Chronicle.*

Once past the lighted dredge, he cut all his running lights and made headway in complete darkness toward the gloomy shadow of the Rock. If they were intercepted by the Coast Guard, or worse, if they were caught in the process of making the landing, the skippers could face not only fines and arrest but the confiscation of their boats. This "caper" carried serious risks for the Sausalito Navy, and Peter knew it well enough to have already consulted a lawyer, just in case. The lawyer was Aubrey Grossman.

Peter steered his motor sailer in a slow gliding approach to the lee side of the island. Teft, in his powerfully beamed cabin cruiser, could make twelve knots, far faster than the eight knots Peter could manage in the *Seaweed.* Neither of them had ever gone in closer than the two hundred–yard warning area around the island, let alone landed there. They were uncertain of where to put in. There was a small slip alongside the dock that had been used by the prison boats, but it looked to be in uncertain shape and possibly chained. In any case, it wouldn't allow for a quick getaway. Teft opted for the less tricky, though perhaps more hazardous approach alongside the floating water barge that was tied to the dock. Peter headed in behind him.

Landing at the water barge. *Right to left*: Al Miller, Ross Harden, Joe Bill (with hat and poncho). Photograph by Vincent Maggiora, courtesy of *San Francisco Chronicle*.

Bowen's *Seaweed* bumped gently, bow first, against the row of tires hung outboard on the barge, and he backed the engine down to let her slide into a snug starboard position alongside. "Wait!" he hissed. "Don't let 'em jump until we tie off." He had nightmarish thoughts about one of the over-eager Indians slipping between the boat and the barge and being crushed and drowned at the same time. They held the boat back, unsure about the timing necessary to match the inky swells that brought them up level with the barge and then rode down again along the edge. It was still a matter of catching that rhythm even after Brooks had secured lines fore and aft. Richard and Al both stumbled on to the barge, and the others followed in turn with less daring, almost crawling across, hushing each other as they made their tripping noises.

Occupiers making their way further into the island through a tunnel. November 20, 1969. Photograph by Vincent Maggiora, courtesy of *San Francisco Chronicle*.

Except for the beacon that kept its predictable slow sweep from the top of the island and over their heads, the place seemed completely blacked out. They had expected to encounter Hart's dog, and Joe Bill had come prepared with a pocketful of leftover hamburger to greet his canine friend from the last invasion. But there was no sound, except the clattering they themselves made as they crossed the barge and climbed up on the concrete dock. An old crane, rusting away to orange from its once bright yellow color, squatted like an abandoned obstacle on one edge of the dock. They made a crouching dash for it, ducking behind the caterpillar tracks and looking again for any movement, listening for any sound. Just off shore they could see a small glint of reflection off the low mast of Teft's cabin cruiser, waiting for Bowen to unload and gently guide the *Seaweed* back out into the Bay.

Suddenly, with what seemed like a crack of lightning, a bulb lit up in the little shack at the far corner of the dock, and then a yard light went on, splashing a glare of silver across the last little group sprinting from dock to crane. The Indians froze in their hiding spot. Peter's boat made muffled gurgling sounds as it pulled away from the barge. A tense few seconds followed when they could see someone moving around through the windows in the shack. The figure seemed to be looking out, then moving toward the door. This, they knew, would be the showdown.

In the shack, Glen Dodson stretched his five-foot frame across the counter to get a better look out the window, confirming the chilling glimpse he had of shadows running in the dark across the dock. He was alone on the eerie old prison island. John Hart had taken his dog and gone fishing for the weekend, leaving Dodson in charge with an admonition to the new man not to get jumpy about ghosts. Still fully dressed, Dodson had been drowsing in front of a small TV screen showing an old movie. For a moment he thought, and then he was certain, that he heard a boat engine. His heart jumped and he felt his stomach tighten in a tremble when he peered through the window and spotted the lumpy figures lurching across from the barge. Looters. Thieves, or maybe killers, went through his head. When he switched on the dock light he captured them, roachlike, in their scramble. It was with relief when he realized what he was seeing.

"Mayday! Mayday!" Dodson burst out of the shack, yelling. "Mayday! The Indians have landed!"

"Whaat?" Oakes hoarsely shouted to the others behind the crane, incredulous over what had become of the confrontation they were expecting. Joe Bill's face slowly cracked into a grin wider than the Bering Strait and then exploded into laughter that set off ricocheting giggles all over the tensely stilled dock. Cautiously, and then with more and more confidence, the Indians rose out of their crouches, watching in amazement as Joe in his flat-billed hat and brightly striped poncho strode across the dock to shake Glen Dodson's hand.[2]

Glen Dodson, Joe Bill, Al Miller, and other occupier in the guard shack on the dock. November 20, 1969. Photograph by Vincent Maggiora, courtesy of *San Francisco Chronicle*.

11

Word Reaches the White House

Amid all the tension and excitement it seemed certain Dodson had not reached for his telephone to call for help. Now, in tow under the sheltering arm of Joe Bill, the Indians made certain he would not correct his error as they walked with him back into the guard shack. It was already past 4:00 A.M. At that time of year they could expect another two hours before daylight, but the bulk of the landing party was still offshore or even still waiting at the Sausalito dock for Peter and the other boat owners to make another trip. If the Coast Guard were alerted now, the small first landing party could be cut off, leaving them in much the same situation as they faced on November 9.

Glen Dodson would have to be watched, at least until the boats got everybody ashore. It wasn't that tough of a job. Dodson was a friendly little fellow without the hardcore "con boss" attitude of Hart and other caretakers. It was just a strange watchman's job to him, and it could get pretty lonely. He was glad for the company, and happy to swap jokes with the young Indians who surrounded him in the cluttered little office shack. Besides, Dodson confided to them, he was one-eighth Cherokee himself.

Peter Bowen steered the *Seaweed* around in a short looping circle, checking out the wheelhouse window to be certain it had not all been a trap. He could see several of the Indians on the dock gesturing to him to come back. Except for the light that now made it easier to see the landing, everything seemed under control. He headed back to Sausalito for another load, as Teft nudged his Chris Craft to speed back ahead of him. Beyond that, just coming vaguely into sight, was Mary Crowley's Czech-built vessel, making fine progress under full sail. The boats would make two roundtrips before daylight, putting a total of ninety-two Indians (including two children) on the island. Peter's terror of one of them slipping in their leap to the water

The Sausalito-Indian Navy: Mary Crowley, Brooks Townes, and Peter Bowen on the thirtieth anniversary of the occupation, holding their monograph about the invasion. A joyous day, especially for Peter Bowen, who passed away six months later. Photograph by Judy Rosen.

barge was relieved. None did. But after he had brought out the last group, he tied the *Seaweed* to the barge and decided to go ashore and satisfy some of his own curiosity. Unfortunately, he underestimated the distance in his jaunty step back from barge to boat, and plunged into the Bay himself. Brooks Townes said Peter seemed to "levitate" himself up out of the water and onto the *Seaweed*, his pride being the night's only casualty.

The leading group of Indians—Richard, La Nada, and the others—already knew their way around the island from their explorations on November 9 and 10. So it probably wasn't necessary for Glen Dodson to show them the warmest spots, some even with fireplaces, in the officers' quarters and the stately old warden's residence at the top of the hill. Still, Glen was being helpful in making everybody as comfortable as he could. By the time the leadership group of Richard and Al and a few others settled down on the old carpet liner that was still intact in the warden's living room, they were all convinced that Dodson would present no problem. Someone had managed to build a fairly cheerful little blaze in the fireplace, cutting the chill of the approaching dawn. There was an oddly comfortable sense of victory to it, like accomplishing something in an easier way than you had expected.

Richard grinned at the *Chronicle* reporter and leaned back from his seat on the floor, resting against an edge of the fireplace. "Well," he said calmly, "what time you think they'll get here?"

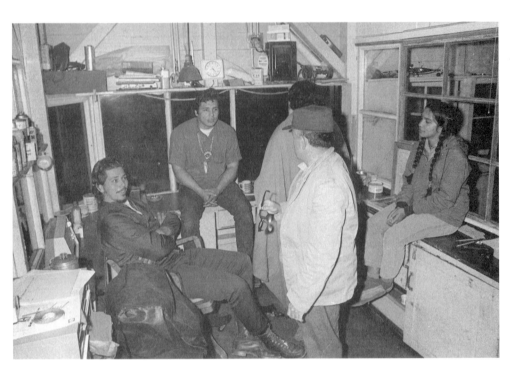

Richard Oakes (seated in center) wearing "borrowed" ivory scrimshaw.
Photograph courtesy of *San Francisco Chronicle*.

"The feds? I don't know. What time is it now?" Findley couldn't help noticing that Richard had added a little decoration to his collegiate apparel of short-sleeved shirt and blue jeans. Around his neck, almost like a talisman of authority, there was what seemed to be a carved ivory horn.

With the exception of John Hart himself, however, the feds did not show up on the island for most of that day, and never, during the many more days to follow, in the force the Indians had expected. Even John Hart seemed resigned when he arrived just after dawn to find the Indians scattered around the floor of the warden's house. Not too grudgingly, he offered to show them where the three working toilets were located on the island, and a few rooms apart from the others where the women and children might find privacy.

For the main group, though, it was still too early to be concentrating on where to settle down. The old prison was a treasure house for exploration, like finding one of those long-lost cities in a jungle someplace, or going through a secret door in a pyramid. The cells stood open on both tiers, as if untouched since they were last emptied. Some of them bore scratchings on the walls in codes and meanings lost to the memories of those who had occupied them, even such legendary people as Al Capone and Robert Stroud. Below the cell block itself the stairwell led down into even more intriguing territory, the hidden reaches of dark solitary cells, and below that down into the deepest blackest holes of the old dungeons. Other buildings still contained machinery and equipment necessary for running what had been a small city unto itself. There were shops and storage areas, lookout towers and gun wells. It was an adventure just to be there, unrestricted from looking into all the island's secrets.

The boat owners and their crews were just as curious as the Indians, and their presence was welcomed in these first hours of unrestrained discovery. Brooks for one remembers that as they landed their last load in the half-light near dawn, he heard some distinctly non-Indian sounding music coming from the dock. Glen Dodson had gotten out his bagpipes to lend a little ceremony to the occasion.

It was later, outside the cell block in the pit-like exercise yard surrounded by giant concrete steps that formed a sort of amphitheater, that Townes noticed the amulet Richard was wearing and recognized it as a scrimshawed killer whale's tooth from Peter's boat. The two young men confronted each other with Findley trying to intervene to prevent a fight.

"Don't get excited," Richard said. "It was a souvenir, that's all. I'll give it back. It's just celebration. C'mon, we WON!"

■

"They made it?!" I whooped into the phone. "Everybody?" All the details Bobbie gathered indicated the invasion had been accomplished without any problems at all. The news was just trickling out from scattered, and some said possibly unreliable reports when she called me at the conference in Minneapolis, but from what she had gathered from all the people in support at the Indian Center and elsewhere, the landing was certainly a huge success.

I rushed back to the afternoon plenary session of the Indian Education Association, nearly spilling the load of Proclamations under my arm. The session was being held in a big auditorium-like room, and the chairman must have spotted me coming with a look on my face that said I had the news I'd promised him. He stopped the session and invited me to the podium.

Exploring. Photograph by Brooks Townes, November 1969.

"I have just learned," I began, still huffing and puffing in my excitement, "that as many as a hundred Indians landed on Alcatraz this morning, and this time, they're there to stay!"

I don't really know what I had expected, but I was actually a little surprised at all the cheering that spontaneously thundered through the room. I tried to read from the Proclamation after I set the big pile of copies up on the dais with me, but people kept rushing up to grab the copies for themselves; I finally just divided them up among the willing hands of two or three nearby volunteers who started passing them through the audience.

Like everyone else, the Indian scholars and educators attending the conference had seen and read of the previous attempts on the island in that month, and had been at least interested in all the colorful and bizarre aspects of an attempt to recapture federal property. Nowhere in the public press that I knew about had anybody condemned the action, or tried to say it was a criminal act or a threat to the government. To the contrary, it was as obvious in Minneapolis as it might have been in San Francisco or Los Angeles, or Pine Ridge, South Dakota, for that matter, that people were enthralled by the idea. Taking back a bitter symbol of repression and punishment for which the United States had no further use was not only appropriate, it was outright daring and inspiring. Most people, I am sure, regarded it as presenting very little real risk to the people involved or to those who supported them. It could end peacefully, but meaningfully, as a symbolic gesture, perhaps, without anybody really getting hurt. On the other hand, something else began to take hold in Minneapolis that day, just as it had all over the country. Alcatraz, they realized, could be more than just a symbol. Those twelve acres in San Francisco Bay could endure for the purposes of Indian people longer than just the afternoon headlines.

That year, 1969, had already set in motion a new momentum that was shaking us all out of the lassitude and indifference toward the attempts at Assimilation and Termination in the 1950s. Richard Nixon's administration had begun with promises from Vice President Agnew himself at the start of the year to support initiatives for Indian self-determination. Agnew had told the National Congress of American Indians meeting in Albuquerque in October that the new administration would end all the old paternalistic policies, including Termination, and listen to the tribes themselves.

"Let us now and forever put to rest all the fears and begin positive action together," Agnew said. "For every Indian problem there is also an Indian opportunity. Building upon that special relationship between Indian tribes and the federal government, we will solve the problems and open the opportunities."[1]

Vine DeLoria, Jr.'s first book, *Custer Died for Your Sins,* was published that year and rapidly became a bestseller. It was carried around and quoted by people at this conference in Minneapolis, itself a milestone in establishing Native American autonomy in education.

In parts of his book Vine was blunt and critical about the failure of current Indian leadership to exploit local situations for national attention, as the civil rights movement had done. He held no real hope for Indians becoming a powerful political lobby or a major influence in the marketplace. "But we will have the intangible unity which has carried us through four centuries of persecution, and we will survive," he wrote. "We shall wear down the white man and finally outlast him. But above all, and this is our strongest affirmation, we SHALL ENDURE as a people."

The taking of Alcatraz, the brash and bold action of young people themselves who were willing to go beyond mere theory and debate, riveted the attention of the public—and rallied support for its still unclear but obviously promising implications about the future.

"Yessir!" people at the conference exclaimed when they shook my hand. "Right on, man!"

Clearly I couldn't take that much credit for a landing that had in almost all its logistical details been pulled off by the students, with Richard as their most visible leader. But at that point I regarded it proudly as the outcome of months, if not years, of work by many of us in what was being called the Indian "community" of San Francisco. That's another of those words that emerged with new meaning in the 1960s. We weren't really a "community," of course, in the sense that we all lived near each other or that we even shared all the same social beliefs and institutions. We were an assortment of Indian people, most of us from distant places, who found ourselves with a common interest in cultural survival. We didn't really even share many of the same customs, except those we knew to be exceptional enough from European culture to be acceptable among us. We had formed an alliance among many peoples whose ancestors might never have imagined it. For that purpose we could accept being "Indians," and if the media wanted to call us a "community" then at least it gave strength to our cause that we had not had before. I could see from the reaction in Minneapolis that Alcatraz was making that community a nationwide reality in a way unlike anything in the past.

Nevertheless, there are still communities within communities. My own cousins from Red Lake never could feel comfortable in all the crush and hustle of urban life, and I understood their feelings. With all the celebrations and congratulations and a couple of news interviews done in Minneapolis, I gladly accepted their invitation to join them in a day or two of hunting snowshoe rabbits back home.

■

On the afternoon of November 20 in Washington, D.C., a news ticker in the office of Leonard Garment, Special Counsel to the President of the United States, typed out a simple bulletin: "Indians Seize Alcatraz."

Bradley Patterson was a career social servant and veteran of the Washington scene who had been assigned only that September as a liaison to Garment's office in domestic affairs. He instantly recognized the significance of the item and carried it in to his boss. Neither Garment nor Patterson had any particular expertise in Indian affairs nor, for that matter, were they up to speed at that time on all the complications about disposal of the old prison island. The capture had implications for the Department of Justice, the Bureau of Indian Affairs, the Department of the Interior, and maybe even national defense. Their hasty research, however, quickly led them to the only federal agency that seemed to have any authority over the island, the real estate–responsible General Services Administration (GSA).

Robert Kunzig, freshly appointed and approved by the Senate as Nixon's chief administrator of the GSA, had already heard about the invasion and was determined to launch prompt, no-nonsense action that would send a message to all potential federal trespassers. He told Garment he had already lined up a force of federal marshals who would remove the Indians, forcibly if necessary, by noon the next day.

Garment and Patterson were appalled. What Kunzig had planned would almost undoubtedly set off a confrontation that might end with bloodshed in what was already probably the most troublesome region of the nation. It could escalate into an international incident. Garment, speaking on behalf of the president, ordered Kunzig to halt all such plans and put him in touch with someone more directly informed about the situation.

Kunzig was furious at this overriding of his authority so soon into the new administration. He told Garment that if it was going to be handled that way from the White House, there was no reason to further confer with him. Instead, he grudgingly suggested that Garment talk directly with his regional administrator in San Francisco, the easygoing agent who was a veteran of the November 10 eviction, Tom Hannon.

"The reason we dealt with him was because Tom would get on the boat and come out to Alcatraz and talk with the Indians and find out how many there were, what their demands were, how many women, how many children—were there armaments, food, water—the whole situation, and then get back to the White House," Patterson recalled.[2]

As it was developing, though, Hannon didn't need to rush out to the island to assess the situation. While Kunzig was trying to organize his counter-invasion of federal marshals, the attorneys alerted by the mainland support group had already been in touch with Hannon. R. Courbin Houchins, who had suggested that we might consider pressing charges against the feds, was joined by Aubrey Grossman, a brilliant legal tactician with years of experience in labor and civil rights struggles.

From the November 9–10 incident Hannon already knew, at least in general, what the Indians were demanding. As he understood it, they felt they had a right to reclaim federal surplus property. Their proclamation on Alcatraz restated all the problems of the island and its run-down condition, and vaguely suggested it be transformed into some kind of cultural center or school. Up to now all of that was beyond Hannon's legal authority even to consider, but Garment and the White House had given him new, if still unclear, power to begin some kind of negotiations with the Indians. This was something Hannon had not planned or prepared for. In talking with the lawyers, all he could agree to was that some peaceful solution had to be found in a manner that avoided a confrontation.

In the meantime, however, while calls went back and forth from and to the White House, news of the invasion was beginning to set off almost a party atmosphere on San Francisco Bay. Newspeople scrambled to hire boats to take them out to the island, and one television crew even landed their helicopter in the lower yard. More than that, though, private boat and yacht owners saw the situation as a virtual open house on mysterious waters that had always been off-limits to all but government vessels. Sailboats of many descriptions and motorized vessels ranging from the size of mine sweepers to outboard dinghies cruised close ashore to the forbidden island. People on the boats threw food and blankets and even cigarettes ashore to the Indians as bribes to come aboard for their own explorations. Most of them were turned back with a friendly wave. There is no doubt that from the beginning there was immediate popular support for the Indian cause, but it was mixed with long-held curiosity about the island itself.

What developed and was described on that afternoon as a Coast Guard blockade of the island was really more of a hastily assembled policing effort by the federal water cops who were trying to direct traffic in what they feared might be a disastrous chain of collisions. In a way, though, the speedy little white cutters with their diagonal red stripe only added to the confusion in a dodging game of maneuver around the newly liberated Alcatraz.

Late that afternoon, about 4:00 P.M., Tom Hannon made his trip to Alcatraz. He was accompanied on the Coast Guard boat by Aubrey Grossman and R. Courbin Houchins. Richard Oakes was there to meet them. He had not slept in two days, and had only tasted at the food being assembled in the Indians' makeshift kitchen. For the most part it was bologna sandwiches. Still, Richard was being fed on adrenaline. He recognized Grossman from an earlier conversation he had with the attorney on the mainland, and Hannon, coming alone without any supporting force at all, seemed to be offering a surrender. Richard was perhaps at his highest moment.

They spoke briefly on the dock. Hannon and Oakes already knew each other, and they had no difficulty coming quickly to terms. Hannon reiterated what he had said before about the island being dangerous and unlivable, especially for women and children. He was probing in part for the sort of information wanted by Garment and the White House, but Richard waved off his offers to help some of them leave, assuring Hannon that they had come prepared to take care of themselves. Hannon suggested that all supplies to the island, including water, could be cut off, but Richard only needed to gesture to the slowly circling flotilla of private boats offshore.

The GSA administrator, always with what seemed a casually friendly demeanor, had no way to know how far his authority to negotiate with the cocky young renegade might go. They spoke for about an hour before they reached a compromise that was supposed to carry through only one more day. Hannon would permit another supply boat to land the next morning, but the Indians must be prepared to leave by the end of that day. Richard, along with Al Miller and two others from the landing party, would go back to the mainland with the Coast Guard boat to discuss it with their support group at the Indian Center.

As the two stepped aboard their vessel, attorney Aubrey Grossman came back off, carrying his sleeping bag.

12

Bluffs and Bombast

HANNON'S BLUFF HAD NO REAL CHANCE of success. In fact, with Grossman now aboard as resident legal counsel and Richard on his way back to the mainland to arrange for new supplies, the position of the Indian occupiers was stronger than ever.

The GSA administrator had to assume from the early news accounts that the Indians had come prepared to stay and probably to resist any attempt to remove them. But the truth was that the big landing that morning had been only slightly better organized than the more spontaneous event on November 9. Food supplies were limited to nothing more substantial than an accumulation of cold cuts, bread, and assorted snack packages, worthy of a large picnic. Some of the occupiers had not even brought along sleeping bags and were sharing what extra blankets could be found. Although Richard and the others tried vaguely to dodge the question, there were no guns or armaments of any kind. The only plan for confronting what all of them believed would be an inevitable assault by authorities was simply to hide.

"We won't physically resist," said twenty-two-year-old Dennis Turner, a Luiseño tribal member and one of those involved from the start in the Little Res. "We're not going to fight them, but how are they going to find us?"[1]

It was that excitement, that game almost, of scattering into the hidden niches and secret rooms of the labyrinth of buildings on the island that still held the attention of most of the occupiers. Richard's meeting with Hannon went unnoticed by the majority of them, and word that there would be another supply boat in the morning spread around the island like a rumor. Richard and Al and the others had not yet convened anything like an organizational meeting on the island. No one was really sure what might come next. In that first day, media people seemed to be swarming everywhere, taking pictures, doing interviews, virtually staging the event for mass release. Crudely fashioned signs began appearing here and there declaring it "Indian Land" or, in more select areas of the cell block or the living quarters, specifying territory like "Paiute Country." There was no order to it all, and no real leadership, but the longer it went on that day the more there was growing confidence, along with growing apprehension, that this occupation would last longer than any of them expected.

That night, as the twentieth century's first recapture of federal territory by Native Americans ended its first full day, forty more Indians landed on the Rock. The Indians no longer hid in the giggling shadows of the old prison island. Someone had found an empty barrel and rolled it up to the tiny courtyard at the top of the hill. In the darkness, around the fire they lit in it, the young people began an incredible Forty-Nine that would last until dawn.

■

Just three days before, Richard hadn't been able to find a boat. Now, he could control an armada, the likes of which had never before been seen on San Francisco Bay or probably any place else. Publicity about the landing had generated what could fairly be called a frenzy of support. It didn't matter whether people were inspired by the Indian cause or satisfied that it might block Lamar Hunt's plans, or if they were just curious about the island. Everyone, it seemed, wanted to be part of it, and everyone wanted to go to Alcatraz if they could. The Indian occupiers could probably have made a lot of money just charging admission. But they didn't need to go to that much trouble. Cash contributions, along with food, clothing, blankets, and piles of best wishes were already beginning to stack up at the Indian Center. If logistics had been a problem a week before, forming some sort of organization to handle it all was now the most daunting task facing Richard and the mainland group led by Earl Livermore and Don Patterson of the San Francisco Indian Center.

On the island, La Nada had found a place in the old officers' quarters for herself, her sister Geraldine, and her son, Deynon, who would become known as "The Alcatraz Kid." Deynon is the nephew of Russel Means, who had boarded the island with his father in 1964. As fired up as ever by her own political passions, La Nada had taken an active part in painting over the old federal warning signs to read "Keep Off. Indian Property." She had used her own experience from the previous landing to point out some of the best secret hiding spots to others, and she put in her share of time on "KP" duty assembling what limited food the invaders had at the beginning. La Nada's instincts honed at Berkeley always led to some sort of political

The coast guard attempts to stop further landings. Photograph by Brooks Townes.

order and, once again, she could see Richard was being carried away on a media ego trip.

"We didn't have much for setting up an organization other than the way that we had learned from our previous lives," she recalled. "The way that we had lived on the reservations with the tribal structure and then the way we organized in the community, and that's the only organization that we knew. We didn't know much about how to set up a traditional government. . . .

"Unfortunately, along with that was built in a patrilineal system, and so we were mocking what we learned, and even though the women had a strong voice, we wound up doing it exactly the way we did it a long time ago. The women pretty well selected the leaders, and we went ahead and selected Richard to represent us."[2]

In his book *Custer Died for Your Sins*, Deloria points out that nobody elected Crazy Horse; nobody said he was the people's choice. He just was. So Richard just was.

The Coast Guard still didn't have clear orders. Hannon, on behalf of the General Services Administration, had presented the Indians with a sort of deadline to remove themselves from Alcatraz. To the extent they were able to do so, the Coast Guard kept a loose patrol around the island to prevent further landings, although that proved to be almost totally futile.

"I remember my sister and my two aunts and myself were able to get on this tiny, tiny speedboat," said Shirley Guevara, a young Mono from another terminated California tribe. "The guy put us up in the bow and threw a tarp over us, and I remember bouncing over the water and being so scared. And the Coast Guard came after us and stopped us, and he [the helmsman] said to us to be real quiet. And the next thing we knew, we took off and outran the Coast Guard boat and wound up at this huge barge. This guy, Roy, let us off and waited a while, then went back and picked up some more people."[3]

The Coast Guard had only its old rules of keeping boaters away from the island to guide the sailers. Those rules were meant to prevent anybody from assisting an escape from the prison. There was nothing to explain what to do with people who wanted to stay there.

In Berkeley, Peter Jones loaded his strange little motorized sampan with as many friends (including two local Indians) and as many supplies as they could find and set off across the Bay into the crowd of vessels circling Alcatraz for the second day. There had to be some pride at stake as the fast Coast Guard launch quickly maneuvered to cut off the outrageously Asian-rigged vessel headed in for the Alcatraz dock. Jones steered hard to starboard and avoided their first pass, but the Coast Guard launch gunned around in another water-churning attempt to block him. The action drew the immediate attention of the Indians and the ever-present media people on the dock, some of whom started cheering as the strange joust continued among the clutter of other circling boats. Closing in on the sampan, a Coast Guardsman threw a line he hoped would wrap around its complicated rigging, but the sampan came back sharply to port, ramming the launch and knocking the crewman off his feet. Hilarious laughter came from shore as someone on Jones's boat tossed over a rubber life raft, followed by two Indians who jumped in it and began paddling to shore. Maneuvered awkwardly close to the water barge and slightly damaged from the ramming, the Coast Guard boat backed off, allowing Jones to pull in close alongside as crewmen threw ashore bags of fruit and vegetables, six-packs of beer, a couple of gallons of milk, and two frozen turkeys. The dock erupted in wild, raucous cheering.[4]

Children with supplies. Photograph by Brooks Townes.

Jones was cited when he returned to his own slip in Berkeley for reckless and negligent operation of a watercraft, but the citation was like a traffic ticket and, just as it had been for many other boat owners daring similar games in those early days, worth the trouble.

Both in the general media and by means of our own informal "moccasin telegraph," word spread that what the Indians on the island needed most was basic supplies—food, water, and power—to sustain their occupation. Less than forty-eight hours into it, the response came with gestures perhaps more generous than they were actually sustaining but, nevertheless, greatly encouraging.

The afternoon of Hannon's implied deadline passed without any indication that the Indians were preparing to leave. To the contrary, there were more of them arriving hour by hour. The population on the island had swollen to at least 150 by the time that supply boat promised by Hannon arrived on the evening of the second day. It was loaded with an astonishing and sumptuous feast prepared by the fashionable Trident Restaurant in Sausalito and its nearby neighbor, the Rock Island Health Food Store.

New occupiers. Photograph by Brooks Townes.

Though they never asked for the credit, it was again made possible by the Sausalito Navy and Mary Crowley in particular.

Once or twice a bright white Coast Guard helicopter thumped overhead in a low pass that seemed intended to acquire some kind of photo reconnaissance. There were little comic encounters between the passing Coast Guard boats and the Indians on shore, meant more to share the overall adventure than to break the tension. "Okay, all you guys get off my island," a Coast Guardsman with a bullhorn ordered with totally unauthorized authority. "Yeah? Get out of our coastal waters," the Indians shouted back with equally unqualified bravado.

The crisis identified at the White House was escalating into a colossal joke on federal authority, shared even by federal agents themselves. Convinced that Hannon and the GSA alone could not simply defuse the situation, Garment and Patterson added William Davoren, the regional coordinator for the Department of the Interior, to the team working for some solution. In a brief joint statement they held off any further federal action for a "cooling-off period" to last until 3:00 P.M. Sunday.

If anything, that uncertain threat was like turning the campus over for a weekend "woodsie." The prepared feast, with wine and trimmings, was delivered in triumph by Richard and Al and the others. It came with drums and cooking fuel and reusable plates, glasses, and silverware. It was a victory banquet.

More than that, the celebration of evident success provided the beginning of much-needed organization that would have time to develop over that weekend. Stuffed and satisfied in glory, the young Indians naturally formed a circle around the cook fire in the theater-like exercise yard. Al Miller surveyed it all with almost unbelieving pride. It was more, much more, than any of them had dared to anticipate, so much more that it had rapidly gone beyond anything they had planned. It was happening with its own momentum, being carried along as if on a high wave, and even now no one had any really certain idea of where it might end.

"We sit here, and some of us can sing these songs in Kiowa or Sioux," he said. "But how many of you can really speak your own language or tell your own history? It's not just the land we want, it's the life."

■

Practical problems lead to political solutions. Isn't that the way it usually works? Staying on Alcatraz, surviving there, required more than just a symbolic intention. In that period of unfettered exploration, the young Indians scattering all over the island had found more than just hiding places. There was abandoned machinery and furniture and even sports equipment in a vintage style few of them recognized. There were vehicles, obviously run out and locked into useless junk that was not worth removing from the island. But with as much ingenuity as Americans were supposedly noted for, a few of the Indians began salvaging parts from one derelict to work on another. A single pickup truck from the early sixties was reassembled from scavenged parts to become a working vehicle before that weekend was out. Others clanking around the old prison trying to discover its workings came up with a system to make more of the plumbing work, at least in a way that would avoid the embarrassing crowds around the more reliable toilets.

Necessity served first in establishing leadership, but politics emerged from success. Well before the new federal deadline of Sunday, a council was formed among the Indians, hammered together and in some ways borrowed and plagiarized from the original Proclamation. Richard and Al were at its core, of course, along with the scholarly Ed Castillo from UCLA and the more nuts and bolts–oriented Bob Nelford, an Eskimo; James Vaughn, a Cherokee from Berkeley; and Dennis Turner, a Luiseño. That would be the first council, but it awarded little credit to the person who was probably most responsible for defining its new purpose: La Nada Means.

While the feds contemplated their next move to address a problem of surplus property and, as they assumed, replacement of a San Francisco Indian Center, the group on Alcatraz devoted their Saturday to creation of an entirely new document, much of it composed for them by La Nada. It would ratchet up the terms by some serious notches and pose a new condition for testing federal resolve.

The new document they presented made two key demands: first, that Interior Secretary Walter Hickel himself personally surrender the island, and second, that the federal government provide enough money in reparation for previous thefts of Indian land to build a cultural and educational center on the Rock that would be run by Indians without government interference. It was Berkeley rhetoric, perhaps, but it certainly matched the government's own bluff.

To Richard, as revealed in one of his many statements to the media, the concept was coming more and more into focus. "It's a place away from everybody," he said. "A place where we can relearn about ourselves and do some new thinking about our future."

In San Francisco, where the support group was increasingly dependent on news accounts about what was happening on the island itself, Earl Livermore was approached for his opinion. "I only wanted a new Indian Center at first," he conceded. "But now, I can see that Alcatraz is important to all of us—not just in the Bay Area—but to all of the Indians. It's unified us like nothing else could do for a century. That's what's really important about it, it's a symbol of our new unity."

The occupation had lasted less than three days. News of it now blazed all over the world. It was taking on international importance as a defiant act of indigenous people. Yet on that quiet Sunday morning in the defiant little patch of lawn that still grew in front of the cell block, La Nada's Alcatraz Kid, Deynon, had found some playmates.

"Wait, wait!" one of the older ones shouted. "I'll be the Indian and you be the federal guys."

13

The Mainland

THAT SUNDAY'S FEDERAL DEADLINE SLID PAST like a hawk on the wind. There were some preparations made on the island to prevent helicopters from landing on the flat, parade ground–like stretch in front of the guards' quarters below the hill-commanding cell block, and lookouts were established to keep an eye out for a possible counter-invasion by sea. But in all the attention that continued to draw support and curiosity toward the occupied island, it was clearly unlikely that federal authorities were going to place themselves in a position of actually starting another "war" with Indians. At most what might happen would be a period of siege that would isolate the bleak and waterless island and gradually force the Indians to leave.

The blockade of sorts continued with its absurd and ineffectual Mack Sennett–style of policing the approaches to and from the Rock. The government still had no accurate number of how many Indians were there at any given time. So many landings and departures slipped past or around the Coast Guard net that monitoring the situation was like trying to keep count on a spawning run. If some of the local yachtsmen might have been turned away, no one was actually being arrested or taken into custody, and many were getting on and off the island without being spotted at all. The most remarkable success at "commuting" to and from the island in those early days was earned, not surprisingly, by Joe Bill.

"They thought he must have had a kayak hidden in the rocks someplace," one of the occupiers laughed. "He was always reappearing to them at Fisherman's Wharf or back on the island like he was two people or something. It was actually just a little rowboat he kept under the dock. He'd get in and lie down flat in it and just float right past them."

The Sausalito Navy, still actively running supplies and more Indians to and from the island, began devising its own techniques for playing the cat

Another landing. Photograph by Brooks Townes.

and mouse game with the Coast Guard, particularly at night. In one case they tossed over an old life jacket soaked in diesel fuel and torched it. While the Coast Guard went to investigate, the Navy went on without lights to the island. At other times decoy boats were used to draw the attention of the Coast Guard in one direction while a loaded boat sheltered by background lights from the opposite shore went in behind them.

On the island some of the giddy excitement of exploring all the new places was wearing off. In a pragmatic way that didn't need structure to find volunteers, jobs and tasks were assigned. A working kitchen was assembled, a pattern found for sharing what facilities still worked, even a day room established in an attempt to keep track of the growing number of kids. Gradually, and by necessity, some order was established and meetings were organized to form a roughly democratic process of decision making.

Federal authorities, still trying to establish some strategy for dealing with the occupation, did not even produce a formal news release on the situation until Wednesday, November 26. Brad Patterson, the White House assistant who had inherited the leading role in finding the right federal response, remembers that although the news release came out officially from the General Services Administration in San Francisco, it was actually written in Washington.[1]

"A group of sixty to seventy young Indians including women and children, from different schools and community organizations in the San Fran-

Children playing on the island. Photograph by Brooks Townes.

cisco Bay Area, is demonstrating on Alcatraz Island to publicize their demands for an educational and cultural complex controlled by Indians," the news release began.

> There are health hazards on the Island, and the General Services Administration is concerned for the safety of the Indians there. The sanitary facilities are minimal. There is inadequate shelter from the elements and the cold night air is conducive to colds and more serious discomforts. . . . Since the demonstration has remained peaceful and orderly, the use of force to remove the Indians from the Island has been avoided.
>
> The Indians on the Island have asked Secretary of the Interior, Walter Hickel, to meet with them on Alcatraz but only with the precondition that Alcatraz be donated within two weeks to an Indian controlled entity and that a 'major university and research and development center' be funded by the

United States without any Government participation in the administration of this entity.

Secretary Hickel has announced his willingness to "meet with their representatives to discuss their views on what should be done with the property," but without any conditions in advance of those discussions.[2]

The news release concluded by saying that GSA Administrator Tom Hannon "is urging the Indian group to leave Alcatraz Island and to enter into discussions with an interagency group in San Francisco, with good faith pledged on both sides."

Written in Washington, D.C., three thousand miles from the "group" that was "demonstrating" on Alcatraz, the news release was certainly not meant to be as humorous as it was read in San Francisco. At least, though, it was in keeping with the spirit of the drama.

■

Renewed with my own sense of being part of the natural land (although usually a little beyond range of a fleeing rabbit), I arrived back in San Francisco that Monday. It was like coming back to find that a seedling you had planted only a week before had already sprung into a tree and was beginning to bear fruit. The San Francisco Indian Center, just a temporary storefront shelter when I left, was now a busy hive of activity, organizing and reorganizing itself to meet the steadily increasing demands of more Indians wanting to go to the island and more and more non-Indians offering contributions of food, money, and piles of clothing that seemed to make no useful sense. Where once we had used every means we could think of to attract media interest, now there weren't enough people prepared to handle all the requests for interviews and photographs. People I had never met and didn't know were somehow in charge, at least from a media perspective. Dean Chavers, a young Lumbee with academic credentials and a white-shirt-and-tie professional appearance, had sort of taken over the role of spokesman, more like a career public information officer than in the spontaneous way we had handled it before. Dean looked white and carried himself in a business-like fashion beyond what I expected. Charles Dana, more obviously Indian in his appearance, seemed to be coordinating truckloads of logistical details like an experienced foreman. He walked with a congenital limp that drew attention to all the work that seemed almost unfairly imposed on him. I didn't know these guys, and they didn't know me. It wasn't like I felt myself to be the victim of some kind of palace coup that had occurred while I was gone, but it was confusing to see how rapidly people had

Alcatraz has become a tribe of its own. Indian people and their supporters. Photograph by Ilka Hartmann.

appeared to take on jobs that needed to be done. I had to reestablish my own role in deciding what this was all about.

"It's unbelievable, Adam. I don't know where they're all coming from," Don Patterson told me. "It's like a revival or something."

In just the brief, dramatic act of seizing the island and holding it for less than a week, Alcatraz was no longer just a barren relic of penal cruelty. Alcatraz had become a tribe of its own, and it was as if it had summoned up the spirits of Indian people who were thought to have vanished forever.

"There was a kid who arrived this morning from Texas who told me he wanted to join his people," Don explained. "I asked him what tribe he was from, and he said, 'Comanche.'"

We were always looking for homeboys or girls from Oklahoma. So we asked him where he was from. Anadarko? Lawton? He didn't even know those names. So we said, well, what's your hometown? And he said, "Pasadena, California!" And when did you find out you were Comanche? He said, "Last Wednesday! Me and my family were watching the news and I blurted out, 'I wish I were an Indian. I'd go to Alcatraz!' That's when my

An exuberant young woman flashes the peace sign. Photograph by Ilka Hartmann.

mom said, 'Son, you are an Indian. You're half Comanche.' So I packed up my stuff and came."

There were suddenly lots more Indians, and lots and lots more people with "Indian blood" than we had ever met before. But it didn't matter so much whether the stories were all true, or whether all of the people coming to support us really understood what they were saying. What mattered was that they identified themselves with the cause of Indian people. They knew they were taking a side in all this, and it was apparent to all of us in those early days that, by numbers alone, our "side" was clearly winning. We had not had much experience in handling such success. We were to find that it is not as easy as it seems.

All the accounts of the occupation stress the drama and even the daring of the young students who carried it off but, as I suppose it is with all such historic events, the real work to make it possible was left to a lot of unsung people who seldom had time to share in all the celebration of it.

Dorothy Lone Wolf Miller, a Blackfoot, was one such person without whom the occupation would have ended much sooner than it did. By the beginning of that first full week her offices at the Scientific Analysis Corporation on California Street had been converted to a nerve center for the occupation, a place apart from all the media attention and posturing at the Indian Center. Like the rest of us who would compose the core group of support on the mainland, Dorothy was beyond college age and far more focused than to simply regard what was happening as a mere prank. She realized well before the rest of us that if the occupation was to succeed beyond being a brief media sensation, it would need a firm and quietly constructed foundation of support. It was Dorothy who set up an account at the Bank of California to handle the surge of financial contributions. She formed the books for "Indians of All Tribes," as the Alcatraz occupation now called itself, and, even when the leaders on the island seemed to regard the accounting as an insignificant detail, Dorothy diligently worked to begin and maintain a clear financial record. Using her own experience with business proposals she obtained a grant that would be used to establish an educational system for the children on the island, with Indian women serving as teachers.

Probably most important, however, Dorothy quickly realized that the enthusiastic young people would overlook the serious hazards to their health in the deep chill and unsanitary conditions of an extended stay on the island. With the help of Dr. George Challas and Nurse Jennie Joe, she established a system to regularly monitor health care and dispense what medicines would be necessary. The two-way radio link she established for emergencies between the island and the mainland was the first, and for a long time the only method of maintaining twenty-four–hour contact with occupiers.

Peter Blue Cloud, a young poet with a sense of mature wisdom that seemed beyond many of the other students, manned the radio most hours, and later, with Dorothy's help, formed an island newsletter to be distributed to tribes and supporters all over the nation. The twenty-page booklet, "Indians of All Tribes News," was itself a remarkable achievement in those early days for its compilation of Indian issues and points of view that ranged far from its center at the symbolic heart of a new movement. The writers, in addition to Blue Cloud, bespoke by their names the pantribal sense of it all: Woesha Cloud North, Young-Robbed-Bird-Free-At-Last, Wolf Running, Denise Quitiquit.

So much of the new thinking, the ideas, and the spirit that began flowing from Alcatraz was actually made possible by Dorothy Miller's tireless work, yet she asked for no recognition and received almost none. Except, perhaps, from the federal government, which thereafter withheld research grants from her firm for a period of some five years. "What the hell," Dorothy would say later. "It was a price I had to pay for freedom."

In many ways others, even among us, searched to find our own contributions that could be as meaningful as Dorothy's. Some searched too hard in the wrong directions.

The obviously well-to-do white woman from Sausalito who motored her sailboat loaded with food, water, and even a financial donation into the Alcatraz dock in that first week was welcomed as a benefactor at first. But as time went along her frequent visits and extended stays began to draw attention. Word began to spread among the women that the lady in her skin-tight white sailing slacks found her pleasure with several of the young Indian men. Others noticed that her gifts began to include alcohol and what was suspected as drugs.

Georgia Tachahagachile, one of the more mature women on the island, told me she and others felt they had no choice but to finally take some action. "The next time she came and jumped out on the dock in those white pants, some of us saw her coming and picked up some sticks." In traditional fashion, the wronged Indian women charged with a barrage of obscenities and switching sticks that sent the confused Sausalito lady toppling off the dock and into the Bay. Embarrassed men standing nearby helped her out, but she was never seen on the island again.

In the rush to share this unfolding piece of history, there were also, of course, the preachers. They have always managed to find Indians somehow, no matter where we go. Two Bible-thumpers arrived at the island one day claiming their well-worn books were the only credentials they needed to go among the "heathens," preaching the gospel. My old Hawaiian friend, E. E. Papke, and his brother, Ike, happened to be on the dock that day. Papke, a former guard at San Quentin, was a great grizzly of a man, weighing over three hundred pounds, and his brother wasn't much smaller. But, like many big men, they took a normally quiet approach to life's little problems. There was just one thing that was bound to set something off in that Hawaiian character though. It was being called a heathen.

"If you people are true Christians," Papke fumed as he walked his steady, dominating pace toward them, "you will leave this island, and these people, ALONE!"

The self-proclaimed "minister" took a small step back, but he knew he had at least federal sympathies, if not for sure heavenly intervention on his side for not being physically hindered. "We have a right to be here," he proclaimed, "and we are not leaving this island until we have the opportunity to preach the gospel to the heathens."

There it was again. That word, like an ice pick in Papke's heart.

"You're leaving!" the huge Hawaiian announced, taking a firm grip on the back of the minister's britches and lifting him so only his toes touched the ground on the way back to their boat. His fellow Bible-toter followed meekly along. As the two of them set off at last in their small vessel, Papke shouted one last message. "If you want to complain to somebody about this," he yelled, "tell 'em it wasn't an Indian who threw you off the island, it was two Hawaiians!"

Those sorts of things happened, as people, some of them well-meaning and some of them not, tried to come on board to all the attention Alcatraz was receiving. But in those early days far, far more people with genuine hearts and generous intentions were offering to do whatever they could to help in an action that had captured their imaginations and perhaps a chunk of their consciences.

For us, well, heck, for me in particular it seemed like the perfect opportunity was right before us. I can't recall how many times the question came up for me during my boarding school days at Pipestone, but I'm sure that on at least ten separate occasions I was puzzled over the meaning of that November holiday. After all that had happened before, why did the Indians feed starving white pilgrims? And after all that happened after, why do we re-create the same feast every year, like a national holiday to celebrate missed chances? When I was a kid Thanksgiving seemed like the only time of year when Indians were portrayed as good guys instead of crazy savages. It was sort of an annual truce, like Hanukkah in Jerusalem or Christmas in Belfast.

Alcatraz and Thanksgiving just seemed to fit together like Philadelphia and the Fourth of July. Only this time, who was going to feed whom?

Thanksgiving dinner being unloaded. Photograph by Brooks Townes.

Prayer: Samu Huarte. Photograph by Brooks Townes.

pace that was different, the strolling through the cell block, arm in arm like attentive touring parents come to see the accomplishments of their young.

Many carried dishes and pots of their own to that walled pit of an exercise yard behind the cell block: fry bread and mutton, venison and corn, food for the feast that came with personal attention and meaning beyond the meal itself. By the time the boat from the Bratskeller arrived, brimming with roasted turkeys and trimmings of the finest imagination, as many as four hundred Indians had gathered on the island, an assemblage unlike anything ever before seen in the recorded history of San Francisco Bay.

The pipe passes from hand to hand. *Left to right*: Joe Seaboy (Sioux), Adam Fortunate Eagle, Ed Castillo, Richard Oakes. *With back to viewer*: Elmer St. John (Sioux). Photograph by Brooks Townes.

Among those treasures retrieved for this occasion was one of special importance to me. A few years earlier, my Aunt Anna had solemnly presented me with the ceremonial pipe used by my great uncle, a religious leader among our Red Lake band. The pipestone bowl was wrapped in softly cured moose hide, with the bowl separated from the stem, and Aunt Anna cautioned me that it must never be used frivolously or shown about as some kind of trophy. I myself carved a new stem for it in an intricate puzzle or mystery design. That pipe was meant only for serious purposes, and Aunt Anna was showing her faith in me by trusting me with it. On Alcatraz, in that yard encased by walls trimmed with rusted barbed wire, I unwrapped it and for the first and only time, lovingly joined the two parts and filled the bowl with tobacco sent from our Native fields.

We had established a small altar on the concrete ground before the feast tables. Richard Oakes, John Folster, George Woodward, and Cy joined me in the prayer and blessings for that day. To Grandfather in the heavens, creator of all things. To the east, which symbolizes wisdom; to the south, the west, and the north. And to our earth mother. And then to colors of the people—red, yellow, black, and white—I directed my great uncle's pipe.

Dancers lining up to eat. Mike Jackson, foreground, and Leonard Harrison (both Navajo). Photograph by Brooks Townes.

Never before in any federal prison had Indians been allowed to practice their religion. Even then, in most institutions and on some reservations the practice of Native American religion was banned. But amid the hushed crowd of people strangely contrasted to their bleak surroundings, the pipe passed silently from hand to hand, relit in the chilly gusts as it made its circle among young and old, among people from all the directions and from all the colors of creation who had been part of making this possible. There is no anger in such a moment, no room for hate or bad thoughts. It is a time only for good hearts, for respect, and for trust in the faith that binds us all. When we had shared that one filling of the pipe among as many as we could, I saved the ashes and then separated the red stone bowl from the stem. I gave the stem to Cy as the greatest honor I could bestow on my old friend. The pipe has never been used again.

Should I not have felt proud?

■

There had to be another line after that, of course, along one huge curving buffet to load up with food on the paper plates and utensils provided by the Bratskeller. But what a happy line it was, chatty and well fed already on what seemed to me the biggest and best family gathering of all time. The drums began to sound, and first the Mockingbird Singers and then the Oklahoma Singers took up the call from the center of the yard. The rhythm and the singing reverberated off the concrete walls, bouncing back and swirling again so you could feel the music in your chest, almost prodding you, demanding that you get up and dance. I watched as Elmer and Martha St. Johns, both highly respected Lakota elders and medicine people, took seats on the high concrete steps, carefully attended to by the young people who recognized their elders' status. I don't know that I had ever seen Elmer or Martha smile with such genuine pleasure.

Cy and Aggie sat next to us, with Cy alertly and eagerly taking in every detail, not wanting to miss a thing.

"What do you think, Cy?" I joked. "This 'Indi-onish' enough?"

He grinned and roughly shook my knee, nearly toppling the plate I was trying to hold in one hand. But there was something in Cy's silence, something a little behind the happiness he tried to show in his eyes, that told me Cy was thinking beyond this day.

15

The Island

IN THE NEXT DAYS AND WEEKS, the business of the Alcatraz occupation would have to find its own order and routine that could establish some serious purpose beyond all the media attention. Between those of us on the mainland and those whose daily life continued on the island, there were perhaps bound to develop separate sets of awareness about how to meet that long-term challenge.

No matter what the government might say in grey-faced warnings and somber statements, we had obviously won. There could be no counterattack or sudden action meant to shift us off the island without risking an enormous national controversy that could question the authority of the government itself. Alcatraz was a surplus island with an ugly past and with no other legitimately claimed future. It should belong to the Indians, people thought. Let them show us what can be done with freedom.

It was, however, that thought, far more than any government threat, that was our biggest challenge. What now?

My youngest daughter, Julie, and her even younger brother, Adam, were among the many teenagers making the pilgrimage to stay a night or two, or longer, on the island. A core group of perhaps fifty who had remained since the invasion were revered already as veterans in a more or less permanent base of occupation. Any tribal member who stayed a full week on the island earned a vote on the governing council, but there was always respectful deference shown to those who had made the first landing. For months to come the numbers of Indians on the island on any given day would vary greatly, and those remaining after nightfall would often number less than fifty. The actual numbers mattered much less, however, than the continued impression, conveyed as much by mainland activity as by the island pres-

Waiting for the boat while the fog comes in. Photograph by Ilka Hartmann.

ence, that the occupation had the unified support of virtually all Indian people. So far, at least, it did.

On the island the task was as clear as the cold, damp season descending from the late false summer familiar to San Francisco Bay. Now, as winter was taking hold, the absence of basic comforts was more and more apparent and more urgently in need of some solutions. The first of several generators brought to the island struggled through endless gas-guzzling hours to provide a minimum of power and dreary light but little heat. Everywhere the tangles of vines and the crumbling erosion of old structures remained treacherous obstacles to moving freely, even to making repairs. In time, thirty-five toilets were put back into some working order, a ten-fold achievement from the three available to those who first landed. But it was pure bravado and mostly bad sense when new arrivals tried to set up some kind of cozy camp in one of the notorious cells with their locks rusted open. The cold still tortured them, gripping at the blankets and heavy quilts, driving most to the warmer shelter of the old wood-insulated barracks or officers' quarters. There was plenty of room in those parts, including three apartment houses, two family duplexes, and the chief medical officer's house in addition to the more barracks-like bachelors' quarters. The more ornate structure of the warden's house at the top of the hill was usually reserved for honored visitors.

For at least as long as anything that needed to be done presented itself with obvious insistent urgency to be pulled out or cut away or patched with some available material, there were plenty of volunteers ready to work tirelessly, even warming themselves in their labor. But there was more that called on the imagination as well, much more that demanded some decisions be made and some organization be put into planning. Safety was first. New people arrived every day, eager to explore for themselves the wild ruins. They had to be warned, cautioned, and even restricted from the dangers of some disastrous incident that might serve as a catastrophic ending that the government seemed to foretell. We dared not risk serious injury or an outbreak of illness that might prove them right. And it wasn't just the Indians who occupied or visited the island who made the risks so great. The media had been almost unrestricted in the first days, allowed to see and record for themselves the abandoned and deteriorated condition of Alcatraz. As the occupation became more secure, the media became an intrusion and a hazard itself. They wanted to see what the Indians were making of the place, but they peered into private places as if they were loose in a zoo. They climbed the rotted stairways and rusted catwalks looking for better angles and risking their own safety without concern for what an accident might mean to us. It was much the same with non-Indian visitors who had been granted generous access to the island at first in thanks for their help, but who, as the days progressed, became more reckless and less respectful of our purpose.

So it was that on the island the first priority had to be the creation of some sort of security to protect the safety of those who were there and the integrity of their purpose. In the original documents claiming rights to the island, I had jokingly provided for creation of a Bureau of Caucasian Affairs, or BCA, whose job it would be to administer the day-to-day dealings with the outside world. Joe Bill, I think, was actually its founding member on the island, but even his unstoppable good nature could not soften the fact that the primary task of bringing some control over what had been won was seriously beyond a joke. Alcatraz security would rapidly evolve into jean-vested uniforms with red lettering, strong young men with eyes intent. It was meant to establish their authority, not their accountability.

The concern all outside observers, from boat captain Peter Bowen to the office of the president, had about the presence of children among the occupiers was made a mute point from the time the Alcatraz Kid took his place in the invasion. Within a week or so there were kids everywhere on the Rock, fearlessly and frighteningly going off on little pack discoveries of their own. The adults immediately knew that some sort of structure needed to be established for the children and that, in fact, attention to the youngest among them would help establish the case we were trying to make for Alcatraz as an Indian educational center.

By the second week in December the Big Rock School had opened for the student body of twelve full-time students on the island. Actually, the young Indians occupying Alcatraz were probably better prepared to accomplish that task than any other. They were students themselves, familiar with the neglect of true American history and cultural diversity in their own studies. Some had even had experiences in Indian boarding schools, where part of the intention of education was to make them forget their own history and their own languages.

Now, in a place so symbolic of repression, young teachers took charge with a spirit full of hopes and dreams. Even as late as 1969 Indian schools all over the nation still held their mission to be partly that of stifling tribal tradition, overcoming what the white educators viewed as "superstition" and "aboriginal" culture. Indian children still felt a heavy hand in that method. Beatings and other uses of corporal punishment were still part of a system Senator Edward Kennedy earlier that year had called "a national tragedy—a national challenge."

Among our people, children are not spanked or physically punished. Traditional Indian people believe that the practice is barbaric. Children are allowed their own expression and given direction that is unlike the white way of rules and punishment. With such kindness and understanding the Big Rock School began with instructors such as Linda Aranaydo (Creek), Vicky Santana (Blackfoot), Douglas Remington (Ute), and Woesha Cloud North (Winnebago) working with aides Justine Moppin (Mono) and Rosalie Willie (Pomo). Others, many of them still teenagers themselves, volunteered in a system that stressed remarkable individual attention to the students. They were taught the fundamentals found in any public school, but they were also given a perspective on history and the times that reflected their own cultures. Working with such young people in that way was a completely new approach, an experiment perhaps, the results of which have yet to be known.

Earl Livermore was so taken himself with what he saw of the school in one of his visits to the island that he decided to resign his job as director of the San Francisco Indian Center and move to Alcatraz where he could devote his time to passing on his own skills as a noted Blackfoot artist. Oth-

Meade and Noreen
Chibetty, Comanches
from Oklahoma, on
Alcatraz in 1970.
Photograph by Ilka
Hartmann.

ers, like Meade Chibetty and his wife, Noreen, provided regular instruction
on dance and music, calling upon Meade's nationally recognized experience
as a fancy dancer who had won national honors as early as 1939. Francis
Allen (Sac and Fox) taught Native American arts such as beadwork, leather
working, wood carving, and costume design. A Tlingit from Alaska carved
miniature totem poles. It was a widely varied curriculum, too much, really,
for the children alone, and perhaps more ambitious than it was yet organized.

A communal kitchen, based from the start in the old cell block but soon
moved down to the apartment building, managed handily with butane
stoves and food lockers stuffed with dry ice. There was a daycare center and
nursery for the youngest children run by Maria Lavender (Yurok) and Lou
Trudell (Sioux).

The main cell block. Photograph by Ilka Hartmann.

These things, the accomplishments made so quickly on the island, were convincing even to those who had been skeptics of the earlier actions. Lehman Brightman had stood apart from us when we called for the invasion, but now he proclaimed it the most important action of Native Americans in the twentieth century. Stella Leach had expressed resentment at first for plans she felt did not give enough credit to the 1964 action in which she worked with McKenzie, but now she, along with Registered Nurse Jennie Joe, put her skills to work in a clinic open daily to monitor health needs on the island. Mainland doctors, including David Tepper, Robert Brennan, and Richard Fine, volunteered their regular visits to the clinic.

Two boys playing in the main cell block. Photograph by Ilka Hartmann.

So much was going on at Alcatraz that it really amounted to a second and entirely new phase to our claim of recognition. What was happening on the island truly did amount to the creation of something unique in a pan-Indian movement, beyond any old alliances or conferences or tribal congresses. The Alcatraz experience was alone to itself.

Those of us on the mainland, however, remained more in day-to-day touch with the slow process of educating the non-Indian world about what it all meant. Journalists and commentators still sought what they imagined to be telling references for explaining it all. It was good that at last the general public was beginning to hear and read about Chief Joseph or Red Cloud or Sitting Bull in ways that led them to new understanding. But unconsciously in their good intentions the writers and the commentators still wanted to understand us in the context of white history about Indians.

I made a few trips to the island in those early days to escort some celebrity or another, and there were many eager to go. I would find them always trying to fit the Indian experience into something they thought they already knew about spiritualism or customs. More, I think, than was felt among the people on the island, we on the mainland were aware that people still wanted to understand Indians as if they could place them in the context of the previous century. If this was sometimes laughable among some of us older Indians, it was also sometimes disturbing when these people would come to a new awakening by meeting the younger Indians on the Rock and end by concluding that they had cut themselves off from that past altogether. You could in some ways feel you were leaving history on the mainland and finding the future on Alcatraz. But that was another sadly incorrect illusion.

I was eager to hear firsthand from my daughter, Julie, and my son, Adam, about their experience of staying on the island after Thanksgiving. Both of them had come back almost cocky proud about it. Julie said she and her girlfriends found a cell in "D" block and decided to spend a daring night there, tying the door shut with blankets for protection. In the morning they found their improvised lock untied and Julie's camera gone, but it didn't dampen her enthusiasm for the day's adventuring that followed. Young Adam was delighted to tell of his trips into secret rooms and scary stairwells. There were some problems, "a few bad apples," as Julie said, but there was so much more pride.

16

An "Impressionist" Alcatraz

I THINK IT HAS TAKEN THE PASSAGE of some years and more life experience for those of us who were at the center of it all to gain a little better perspective on how quickly and how naturally the "movement" of Indian Alcatraz grew. There is still always a misunderstanding people have today in trying to explain it or describe it in terms of the "leadership." Some of what I have heard in the years since is an absurd fabrication that seems to have been made up as if it were necessary, the only way to make sense of what happened. For instance, there was the idea that somehow the American Indian Movement (AIM) was behind it all and directing all the action from behind the scenes. I have heard myself described by the FBI as an AIM activist and officer, and by some misinformed Indians as a renegade from the AIM organization. AIM, of course, had nothing at all to do with Alcatraz and, as far as I know, didn't even have any representatives in the Bay Area at the time.

Others have continued believing that it was the pure charisma of Richard Oakes that brought the students into a unified action. Richard was important to it all, and undoubtedly inspiring to many, but his role was more that of serving as a recognizable front for a number of others who did most of the planning and organizing. I, too, have been both praised and criticized for what is often an exaggerated or misunderstood view of my role. In retelling a story in the non-Indian community there always seems to be a need to have a central character—a hero—around whom all the events can be told. It wasn't that way. Indian people didn't "join" with an Alcatraz "movement" because of any organization or any individual. Many Indians who played important parts in the invasion and occupation never knew Richard or me or La Nada Means, or any of those whose names would be most associated with it. The truly remarkable thing about Alcatraz, especially in the

Indian man on his way to Alcatraz Island. Photograph by Ilka Hartmann.

early months, is that what was really happening had almost nothing at all to do with leadership.

It has only been in very recent years that Jerry Hill told me the story of how he became involved. I think it expresses a lot about the often-asked question of what life was "really like" on Alcatraz in those days.

■

Coming out of the Air Force in 1960, Jerry found himself discharged in southern California, a young man still uncertain about what he wanted to do with his life but unwilling to leave behind all the adventures and excitement unfolding before him and return to his own Oneida reservation in Wisconsin. In the sixties, the Oneidas were one of the tribes named on that quietly compiled doomsday list federal authorities had in mind for Termination. Oneida tribal leaders told me years later that they regarded themselves as being at the top of the list in 1969, next in line to be terminated as a sovereign people. It was ironic, but fateful, that in that year one of their own tribal members, Robert Bennett, was replaced by Louis Bruce, a Mohawk, as Nixon's Commissioner of the Bureau of Indian Affairs.

Jerry had not been home often in those nine years since the Air Force, and he was not particularly informed about the issues of Termination threatening his own tribe and his own family. He had found a good job as a hair stylist in Los Angeles, working in a fashionable orbit near the glamour and wealth of Hollywood. It was a good life, with promise. He never tried to hide his own Indian heritage. If anything, he found the instinctive curiosity of people useful; they were ignorant in their way of trying to show it, perhaps, but still well meaning about wanting to know him. He learned of the invasion of Alcatraz the way most people in Los Angeles did, by the newspaper stories and by the television accounts that followed as the first sensational stunts became more and more seriously purposeful.

"Hey, Jerry," he remembers his coworkers teasing him with grins behind the headlines, "you gonna go join your people, Jerry? You gonna split to Alcatraz on us?"

This was joking among friends, not meant to be as racist as it sounds now, but his coworkers were unaware of the feelings sparked in Jerry by the same headlines they mocked. On his days off in that November of 1969, Jerry began taking the long drive up Highway 101 to San Francisco. He wanted to see for himself what was going on with Alcatraz. There was no problem visiting the Indian Center and the island. He was an enrolled tribal member, immediately welcome in ways he had never before experienced.

He made four such trips, each time returning with something intangible that always drew him back. "I was just an observer. I just wanted to see what was going on," he said. "I had never really heard this kind of 'nationalistic' talk about Indians and I kind of thought it was just a bunch of bullshit. But, each time, I would meet some particular person, and they were sort of mentors to me. Peter Blue Cloud, the Quitiquits, Vicki Santana, Dagmar Thorpe, La Nada, that Eskimo guy, Joe Bill—just people I met and talked to. I don't know. The place just started to grow on me."

Now, these many years later, when I think about those whom Jerry identified as his mentors, I see a picture drawn of how those times were taking shape on Alcatraz. Peter Blue Cloud, the artist and poet. A deeply sensitive and kind man who drew great hope from the spirit of the island that he depicted in his own drawings and writings. The Quitiquits, a Pomo family with active traditional ties to their own reservation but with equally deep intellectual curiosity. Dagmar Thorpe, granddaughter of the great Sac and

Fox athlete, whose own life had drifted far from Native American affairs and then turned slowly back in a natural arch through her experience with VISTA and finally to Alcatraz with her mother, Grace. La Nada and "that Eskimo guy," Joe Bill, unmistakable as characters on the island and as the sparks of energy that kept it going. Jerry met Richard, too, and Al Miller and the others so publicly recognized, but what drew him back each time were the individuals in whom he saw himself. He would be connected to them for the rest of his life.

Right after Christmas 1969, Jerry surprised his girlfriend and his co-workers by quitting his job and announcing that he was moving to Alcatraz. "It just finally got to be something I felt I had to do," he said.

He waited, as he had at earlier times during his visits, for the last evening boat to leave Fisherman's Wharf for the island. By then landings after dark had been stopped, both to reduce the chance of accidents and to avoid running a shuttle from the mainland bars. Jerry rode out on that last boat of the evening, meaning to make this trip the beginning of an indefinite stay. Others had made the same decision for reasons of their own, but few who were not students came as Jerry did, with his savings and his car and other possessions stored intact on the mainland as a safely closed chapter on his life.

"It was sort of weird. I got there, and I found myself standing on that lower courtyard, smoking a cigarette, and it was as if everyone had just disappeared. There was nobody to tell me where to go or what to do, and I just sort of stood there thinking, 'Damn, what now?'"

Finally, one of the occupiers came across the lonely figure of Jerry standing on the dock, still lugging his small suitcase and a sleeping bag. They talked, and Jerry was invited to join his new friend and his family in one of the cottages. It had a fireplace, with a cheering blaze in the hearth. Not a bad beginning.

Oneida though he certainly was, and inspired as he had been, Jerry was also a mature young man in his thirties with a certain worldly curiosity that followed in the vein of poets and authors from his own "beat" generation of Americans in search of themselves. Part of him still suspected that behind the shallow front, what was going on on Alcatraz would turn out to be part of some kind of scam.

"I mean, the so-called 'leadership' was always kind of off and running somewhere, and it seemed like everybody was playing to movie stars and the celebrities that would come around, like Anthony Quinn and Jane Fonda, and people were always wondering about what was happening to all the money that was coming in. There was always this sort of infighting. But there was nobody telling you what to do or anything. You just got up when you wanted to and went to see what they had for breakfast or whatever.

There was always something to eat, although it occurs to me now that we had balogna sandwiches a lot."

Once a newcomer had satisfied his or her own curiosity with the inevitable exploration of the island's mysteries, there was little left to do that wasn't self-assigned or just invented from whatever ideas the island spawned. Jerry found a room in the bachelor's dormitory that was littered with piles of old books. "I just kinda gravitated up there and started organizing the books. And then I asked around if there were maybe some kids who wanted to do some reading. They were donated books, I guess, but it just looked like somebody had gone in there and tipped over the shelves and left them scattered around. Everybody was just kind of running loose like that."

Jerry occupied part of his time with his library, taking his place in the island's education system. But there was an almost endless realm to explore on the island. Even places known in the daylight took on new shapes after dark. Shadows crossed the light in startling ways, and sometimes others on explorations or playing some kind of games of their own seemed to create an entirely new atmosphere. Once or twice Jerry ventured down into the thick darkness of the old dungeons below the water line, carrying a newspaper torch that seemed to cast no light, feeling his way along the uneven floor. It was adventure, a kid's game of seeing how far you dared go. But Jerry also noticed some of the more veteran occupiers sorting more carefully through what they had found, especially, he noticed, for the copper wire that could be salvaged and sold on the mainland for a tidy profit.

His own time wasn't spent continually on the island. Periodically he would take the boat back to the mainland, recover his car from the garage where he had stored it and perhaps rent a motel room for the night, where he could shower, watch television, and sleep without the noises that seemed always a part of the nights on Alcatraz.

"I needed those times to sort of 'decompress' for a while before getting back into it. I don't know that I ever did really get into it the way I thought I would, but I always went back. There were things that bothered me there, people who I didn't think had quite the social feeling for being there, you know? But it was a free place; everybody did what they did, and I did, too. It took people who didn't have a whole lot of roots just to be there. It was just that way."

He found himself one warm afternoon sitting on the stone railing in front of the cell block overlooking the lower yard, talking philosophy with a friend who called himself Rock.

"He was a 'Nam veteran, an older guy like me. And he said, 'You know, here we are, and there's maybe only four or five of us on the whole island right now.' There were a lot of places for people to be, and I don't know where everybody was, but that seemed right. It was just one of those times when it didn't seem like anybody else was really there. He was saying how easy it would be for them [the government] to just swoop down in a helicopter and snatch us and close the whole thing down. His point was, 'here we are, just five Indians smoking a joint, and the government doesn't really know what the hell to do about us.'"

Jerry also saw in this freedom a lack of serious organization. He wondered, for example, why in all the time since the occupation began no one had even tried to put up a more serious sign other than the graffiti-like scrawl of red paint that went up in the first days declaring it Indian Land. Jerry thought it was time to put up something better, something that suggested that more than mere vandals were there. He and Rock concluded that this idea was the kind of thing that should be brought up at the meeting of island residents that night and, Jerry said, they went to John Trudell before the meeting began to suggest that John be their spokesman. But Trudell forgot, and Rock told Jerry, "It ain't going to work, nobody's listening."

At that point, Jerry stood up in the meeting to make the point, especially about how easy it would be to land a helicopter in the yard and bring the whole thing to an end. In recognition of how true that was, the council, on the spot, put Jerry in charge of security.

"That was a good lesson for me. I mean, don't speak unless you're ready to take charge. So for a couple of weeks I just did like I had done with the books. I mean, I just tried to do what I thought should be done to put some barrels in the yard and stuff and just generally try to think of what to do, in case. But there was nobody to report to, and nobody really to tell me what they thought. I could call myself Napoleon for all the effect I had, but I didn't really know what to do, and so pretty soon I really didn't do anything."

There was, however, one incident that Jerry recalled from his days on security that was almost cinematically memorable.

"It was just one of those mornings when I was touring down near the dock, and I saw this guy coming up in a row boat. He was obviously a white guy, and a very big guy. I was watching him and saying to myself, 'I hope he don't come over here,' but he was rowing straight toward me. He rowed right up to the shore and got off his boat, and I said 'Hey! You can't come up here!' And he looks at me and says, 'What are you going to do about it?' and I'm thinking, 'shit, there's probably not much I can do.' He started up toward me like nothing could stop him, and he got about ten feet away from me when he stopped all of a sudden and turned around and went

Indians watching. Photograph by Ilka Hartmann.

back. I thought, 'What the hell?' and then I looked back of me and there was about ten or fifteen guys behind me, watching. It was like those old movies when all the Indians suddenly appear at the top of the hill."

For Jerry, the entire experience of Alcatraz was one of almost explosive contrasts between being among what he described as "some of the scummiest, rowdiest Indians I've ever met" and at the same time among "what I'm certain were some of the best intellectuals and thinkers I will ever know. Brave people, accomplished artists and philosophers. People who changed my life. It was magic. Surreal, but magic."

He became close to those who inspired him, like the artist Peter Blue Cloud, and the young women he had met earlier, Dagmar Thorpe and Vicki Santana, all of whom seemed to him to glow with a purpose about it all. La Nada, he had been told, was the "tiger woman" in her burning political commitment, but Jerry found her thoughtful, not just informed, but sure of how to make use of what was being learned, and taught, on the island.

"It was sometimes sheer terror, and it was sometimes something else, something that transcended it all," he said.

There were brutish young men who clearly found their way from the harsh streets of the Little Res in San Francisco or from the turf-conscious neighborhoods of Oakland, to Alcatraz. They came with their street attitudes that threatened others and heightened the tension. They carried an anger about them that was bitter and possessive. You did not cross them, and there was no real organization on the island that could seriously stand in the way of their bullying posture. Jerry had noticed one such young man with a muscular saunter and an attitude that threatened disagreement. He was told there had been some serious fights involving that guy in particular, and he was cautioned to steer clear of those who wanted no part of the intellectual discussion. For Jerry, even as "director" of security, there were just some people on the island whom it was better to avoid.

On a late afternoon, thinking about all those contradictions that still left him uncertainly troubled, Jerry walked past the intersection where the road down from the cell block meets a path into the old shops area on the north end of the island. It was cold, and the light from the west cast sharply distinct shadows like knife blades cutting across the walls of the road and the buildings. The atmosphere was as grim as many convicts must have felt it but, strangely, there was a light melody of music coming somehow from the old building that he knew was still cluttered with parts of machinery and worn out equipment abandoned by the government. It was a hesitant, lilting tune, familiar in some vague way, almost ghostly, but so carefully gentle.

Jerry turned from the path and crossed the concrete walkway leading in to the dimly lit building, its east-facing windows forming a high lattice wall of faded light. Once inside, he could recognize the music as coming from a piano, but being played with a masterful perfection that obviously was meant for the instrument. It drew him in, and he went searching for the source until he saw a large figure hunched over an old upright like those that used to be seen in dance halls. The piano had been left and forgotten there, ignored, Jerry imagined, until now. He came closer, drawing the attention and an easy welcoming smile from the intent musician at the keyboard. It was the bullying young Indian he had been warned to avoid, sitting there alone in that empty building with a nearly worn out piano.

He was playing Debussy's "Clair de Lune."

17

Richard
"And Then There Were . . ."

RICHARD. BY NOW I SUPPOSE everyone knows something of the soaring tragedy of Richard Oakes. His name will always rightfully be the first associated with the historical account of the Alcatraz invasion and occupation. Like other young warriors before him, he blazed so brightly for a while then disappeared, burning up in the friction of the atmosphere.

In the short weeks that followed the great Thanksgiving celebration, the media cast him as "President of Alcatraz." It was their way of finding or inventing new leads and new angles to a story that had generated international attention. Richard accepted the role, but not in the way that many saw it, as being some kind of personal grandstanding and exploitation. From the start Richard had always struggled with his own shyness among people he didn't know. He had been propelled, almost thrust from more informal and intimate circumstances in which he got to know people, a few at a time, into a leadership role. First as the bartender at Warren's, then as head of the small Native American Union at San Francisco State, and finally as a kind of poster image for the drive behind Alcatraz. It had all occurred too rapidly, one event after another, for Richard to have been given even a fair chance at developing a base of leadership that was beyond thin plate. His closest friend and ally, even more than his wife, was the tight buddy he had found at Warren's, Al Miller.

In those early days sooner or later every Indian who came to Alcatraz with any serious intention of staying would encounter and probably meet with Richard. By then he had already become a celebrity, to the media the epitome of the entire movement and a recognizable figure almost anywhere in America. Jerry Hill met and talked with him, and said he was surprised to find that Richard was not so taken with himself, that he was, in fact, inviting, as if looking for friends. John Trudell, who would eventually chal-

Richard Oakes meets with U.S. Attorney Cecil Poole (*right*). John Hart (*second from left*), Alcatraz caretaker, and Dennis Turner (*second from right*), Luiseño Indian and member of Alcatraz Council, look on. Photograph courtesy of Associated Press.

lenge Richard's leadership on the island, met with the Mohawk leader not long after John hitchhiked from Los Angeles to become part of the occupation after Thanksgiving. Trudell's recollection is of being "impressed" with Richard, but he has offered little further explanation beyond that.

However much occurred and developed later, and however it may have been that he was only a figurehead, Richard Oakes was placed in the most uniquely personal position of all on Indian Alcatraz. He had been the young leader recognized at the press party in Sausalito. It had been Richard who read the November 9 Proclamation, and he who had been the first to make the daring leap into the Bay from the *Monte Cristo*. When Tom Hannon came as the federal representative, it was always Richard with whom he met and from whom he took what he reported as the Indians' stance. Richard had a presence in his muscular and handsome appearance that expressed the cause better than I could have or than La Nada could have, or than any among us could have. Without him there might have been an entirely different interpretation of what it was all about.

Richard himself would not have claimed to be an intellectual or even a prominent or well-informed Indian activist. At heart he was a blue-collar person accustomed to hard work and chores, but convinced that those simple ethics could translate into a social cause. Some said he had been raised on the St. Regis Reservation in upstate New York near the Canadian border, and from the time he was sixteen he had worked with his father and his uncles in construction jobs all over New England. In later years, though, I met elders who told me Richard had actually been raised in Brooklyn, apart from his own family. Mohawk tradition that had recently come to disputes over bridges and roads was part of his heritage, but not really in his immediate experience when he came to California to begin an academic career at the age of twenty-five. It is not to criticize Richard, but to understand and honor his memory, when I say that he found himself in a lonely position of trying to fit his own image.

It was not long after the Thanksgiving feast that I was on the island again one day to attend a meeting Richard himself had called. I was on my way up to the theater area of the old cell block when I saw Richard emerge on the spiral staircase leading out of the old fortress area.

"Adam," he called to me. "C'mon up." I had brought with me some fresh clippings from the newspaper coverage of the events, most of them, of course, featuring Richard himself. One in particular went to some length to describe him has "a young Victor Mature" in very flattering terms. In the cluttered little room he evidently used as an office, Richard sat down and studied the clippings carefully. He seemed to have forgotten all about the meeting, and I had to remind him that they would all be waiting for him, more than for me. "Yeah, I know, just let me look at this stuff." He smiled broadly as he read over the Victor Mature reference once again. I just waited, as did the impatient meeting in the cell block.

It would, of course, be Al Miller, the truly trustworthy lieutenant always watchful of his best friend's back, who first noticed that there were serious currents beginning to rise against Richard's acknowledged leadership. "It seemed like the more people we'd get on the island, the more leaders would emerge—people who thought they should be the rightful leader, whether they were in on it from the start or not. Sometimes, people came with their own followers, from their own reservation or their own neighborhood. There was even a street gang who thought they should take over, and they almost did for a while," Al remembered.[1]

With the end of the Thanksgiving holiday, many of the students who had already stretched their break from classes began returning to their campuses. That core group of the invasion was rapidly being eroded and re-placed by other groups of young people without such academic obligations tying them to the mainland. The change was perhaps not so visible as it was visceral, apparent in an attitude less interested in what intellectually might be accomplished on the island than what could be demanded by holding it apart. It was a tougher way of thinking, more street-wise than philosophi-cal, and Richard himself was becoming more and more aware of the chang-ing character of the occupation.

He and Al were on the mainland for two or three days when, Miller re-called, Richard came to visit him. "He told me of this threat to his leader-ship, and he said, 'I don't know how you feel about what's going on.' I said, let me get some guys together and we'll go out there and take care of it, and that's what we agreed on."

It was not meant to be a physical battle, and as it turned out it wasn't. But even Al at the time didn't realize what a collision of forces was represented between the dozen or more young men from the Little Res who came with him and Richard to meet with the roughly equal in number group of young Indian bikers from Oakland who called themselves the "Thunderbirds," and who re-lied for key support on Stella Leach, the mother of one of their leaders.

"The guys said they didn't want a confrontation either," Miller remem-bered. "He [Richard] said, 'We're all Indians,' and I think I kind of played a role of peacemaker to get all of that settled."

But it was not really settled, of course. If anything, Richard knew from the incident that his hold on true leadership of the island was more tenuous than ever. Stella worked actively every day with visiting doctors, respond-ing to medical needs that slowly mounted from the grip of damp winter. This work actually placed her in a more visibly useful position than Rich-ard could hold onto as a media icon, or even in his less celebrated role at the dock, offloading new supplies when they arrived. Frequently he per-formed the deck work with the help of his cheerful twelve-year-old step-daughter, Yvonne.

Annie Oakes had never really liked the idea of her husband becoming so absorbed in this movement on Alcatraz. Among her own Pomo people the island was always said to have been cursed and avoided by others in the Coastanoan tribes as a place of bad spirits. Annie hated the island, and she dreaded all the attention it was bringing for Richard.

■

Sometime before Christmas all of our efforts both on the island and back in the mainland center to establish some clear direction for the occupation

Richard Oakes.
Photograph by
Brooks Townes.

seemed ready to come into some focus. With Dorothy Miller's help we had secured at least one major funding grant of $16,000 from California philanthropist Thomas Mudd, who stipulated that more such donations would depend on his being convinced that money was being administered for worthy purposes related to the occupation. Smaller amounts of money came steadily into the account Dorothy had established at the Bank of California, along with other donations of food and still baffling supplies of clothing that were piling up everywhere. There was, we felt, beginning to develop a hard currency of support sufficient enough to use as a foundation for the next step, whatever that step was actually to be.

A steering committee to administer Mudd's contribution was formed and agreed on. It consisted of myself, Earl Livermore, Dean Chavers, Charles

Dana, and Richard Oakes. Its composition was meant to establish some rough balance between the advice of the elders and the activism we took to be represented by the students on the island but, as money so often does, it proved to be as much of a hindrance as it was any help in organizing. The media was pressuring us now to describe what we intended to do, beyond just rejecting government offers for some kind of negotiated end to the occupation.

Many things, however, were going on that none of us really understood. The power struggle on the island, though subtle in some ways, had planted doubts about the motives of everyone involved. The Bay Area Native American Council (BANAC) was only just then being formed as a way of creating some unified body among the many urban Indian organizations on the mainland. But on the island such talk was regarded with suspicion by many of the new arrivals who believed that the invasion and occupation had been accomplished solely by a student movement. In later interviews even Al Miller characterized the mainland support organization as having been "spawned off Alcatraz." He began to suspect that money was being funneled into the mainland group by government sources to undercut the occupiers on the island.

"La Nada," he told that interviewer, "and I were delegated to go out and make sure the press conferences, if they were given, really reflected what our desires were on Alcatraz." He was afraid, he said, that others on the mainland would "sell us out" for the funding.

The news conference scheduled at the Indian Center in the Mission District before Christmas was meant to address those probing questions about what serious plans existed for producing some viable and lasting purpose for the occupation. I was surprised when I arrived at the center to find a table set up in front of a big hand-lettered banner that read, "Indians on Alcatraz will Rule Alcatraz."

Richard and Al, La Nada, and some others I didn't recognize, had already taken their seats behind the table. Earl Livermore and I stood off to one side, aware of the long glances in our direction from *Chronicle* reporter Tim Findley. He came up to us before the rhetoric-filled news conference was over. "Well, Adam, Earl, it looks like it's over for you guys," he said.

"Yep," we smiled back. It was a hard pill to swallow.

Within the next few days Richard was featured in perhaps his last major interview as the leader of the Alcatraz occupation. He told Lynn Ludlow of the *San Francisco Examiner* that the occupation was "the first time we've gotten all the Indians together. Perhaps we can develop an all-tribes consciousness," he said. The headline to the story read: "Oakes Has One Goal for Alcatraz: Unity."

Not all of the media was taken in by Richard's optimism. Findley especially had been close to it all from the beginning, and it wasn't hard for him to recognize the changes taking place on the island. They weren't subtle differences at all. From a time when non-Indian support had been welcomed, or at least turned away in a friendly manner, there had emerged stories of threats and even extortion demands directed at visiting boats. Bottles had been thrown, bitter, racist remarks exchanged. Findley covered the so-called counterculture as his regular beat; he knew the Marxists from the gangsters. He recognized the players, and he understood the drugs.

"I don't want to do this story, Adam," he told me. "The truth is, I shouldn't be covering this at all. I'm just too close to it. But somebody is going to do it, or something is going to happen that will make everybody do it."

What could I tell him? Tim had worried over the ethical complications of his own involvement in the invasion. Now he was troubled by the obligation he felt to reveal how it had gone sour. I suggested there were still those of us among the older group who understood that it would eventually smooth out, but he told me he already knew of more radical influences that intended to take charge. He wasn't threatening me or us with the information he had, he was agonizing over withholding it. Some on the island especially would always believe he betrayed them. He knew that would be the price he would have to pay.

It was Tim, actually, who first called Vine Deloria. They had known each other for many years already, since the time when Tim was a radio reporter and first gave air time to Vine and his "arrow shirt" sarcasm.

"I was in law school at the time, my senior year, and when I heard about the invasion I just smiled and wished I was through with law school because they were going to need some lawyers," Vine remembered. "But I got these calls from Adam and Tim Findley just sort of harassing me to come out and try to talk some sense to these people and get them to unite. So I came out on Christmas Eve, which I hated. I wanted to be with my own kids."[2]

What Tim and I had hoped for was that Vine could bring a kind of scholarly seriousness back to it all, or at least slow down the spiral that was starting. Vine can be very cynical in his attitude. He is a brilliant, amusing man, but he does not suffer fools. He visited the island several times after that, but he met with frustration. Vine offered to help with a package that would trade the submarginal land of Alcatraz for something more valuable. The Indians on the island said no. Instead he was asked to do an interview about the Rock with Merv Griffin. (So was I, but we both opted out in favor of letting Charles Dana handle it.)

Vine was certainly no "elder" at the time, but he looked with longer eyes at the big picture of what was happening to Native Americans. From the start he regarded the importance of Alcatraz as establishing a new "ethnicity" of Indians, a tradition that was distinct from separate tribal claims. But he, too, was confronted with an unexpected hostility from the younger occupiers when he went to the island that December in an effort to help it find some direction.

"You know, I'd get halfway up the hill there, and somebody would say, 'what are you doing here?' Well, the Bay Area Indians asked me to come out. . . . But that didn't impress them. It was like anyone who didn't swim ashore was really suspect."

Like me in a way, Vine was suspect because he was successful in some other way. Just to prove it, during one of his visits I had him wear my nametag. "I saw all these guys looking at me like that," Vine told another interviewer, "and I said to Adam, 'What's the matter?' He said, 'Well, they threatened to beat me up. They think you're me.' I thought, God, this is wonderful. All the people I've seen on the wharf and then again on Alcatraz, and none of us had ever seen each other before. Kids from all over the country were there, and all of a sudden after two days on the island they were the big radicals and we weren't."

Behind the scenes, something of a power struggle had developed among those of us in the "old" leadership over the administration of that $16,000 from Tom Mudd. Dean Chavers and Richard especially wanted to use it immediately to hire a full-time administrator for the island, but I knew such a plan was unlikely to do more than cause more dissension. This was as close as I came to getting fighting mad at the time before we at last reached agreement that the money would be put in an interest-bearing account for use as emergency scholarship money that could be drawn on by students returning to school. Al Miller's suspicions about government money would later find some grounds, but not then, and certainly not in any way that ever should have drawn disrespect to such an established leader and scholar as Vine Deloria.

For Tim Findley I think the frustration Vine experienced was finally what caused him to go ahead with the story he told both of us he didn't want to do. It was a three-part series. As a result of all the angst he was feeling about seeming to sell out his friends, Findley even removed his byline from it at one point. The series, taking a stinging approach to what had transpired during the month-long occupation, stated that the young Indians had fallen victim to "booze, bickering, and boredom" on the island and that the attempts to establish some form of leadership had become a "Lord of the Flies" struggle between factions. Grimly aware of the ironically racist tone of his words, Findley forecast an end to the occupation based on the last lines of the "Ten Little Indians" ditty: "and then there were none."

After it was published Findley requested to be taken off any further coverage of Alcatraz. He would leave the paper soon anyway, for a stint as an associate editor of *Rolling Stone Magazine*.

In some ways Tim's series was harsher than it needed to be, but in other ways I knew he had additional facts, particularly about drug dealing on the island, that he had not revealed. There was still so much positive about what was being accomplished, despite the troubles, that we all knew it had to continue. The media from then on would be far more skeptical and critical of us, and the government would perhaps begin to feel they had more support for getting tough. But we had to go on, even if that meant that there would be two Alcatrazes—one run from whatever became of the power struggle on the island, and another directed from our continuing efforts on the mainland.

How I wish there had not been the tragic event on which the decision would turn.

18

Yvonne

THE WHOLE BUILDING IS GONE NOW, torn down and pulverized, carted away and scattered as landfill. What tourists see of Alcatraz is what they expect and what draws them there is something of the same curiosity they'd have for a train wreck: the old cell block, sullenly mounted on the top of the hill like the grim bridge of a great ship run aground. If they stayed, though, for any longer than the few hours that visitors do, they would come to the same conclusion that everyone always has about Alcatraz, including the Park Service people who work there now: the cell block is an unlivable place, cold and damp, darkly intriguing at first but inevitably as unpleasant and relentlessly hostile as it was meant to be. Indian occupiers might pose there for the photographers and make a show of being in the forbidding place, but nobody willingly wanted to live there or, after a period of exploration, even temporarily stay there for very long.

The old Devil's Island symbolism of the sinister cell block was in contrast to the simple but still more comfortable construction of the apartment house for guards and employees of Alcatraz. It had that utilitarian appearance of public housing projects built after the war, finished concrete without any real frills, but still suitable, more accepting of light and heat than the chilled tiers of cells on the hill above it. It was in that building where most of the Indians who could not find space in the old wooden cottages wisely chose to stay. It became, as intended, a communal center for the families on the island.

That day, January 3, 1970, the children were playing on the concrete steps with their iron pipe railings that bordered a kind of small interior courtyard to the apartment building. The kids dashed about in what seemed haphazard directions, up and down, chasing and dodging among themselves. At least that's about the best we can imagine of it from what little descriptions we have. Richard and Annie were both on the mainland that day. Others were occupied elsewhere with whatever took up their time on the island. It was the kids who were playing, and we just don't know much more about it, except that somehow on the third floor landing above the concrete courtyard Yvonne suddenly lost her grip or tumbled in some way through the railing, falling those three stories in an instant and landing on her head.

It would have been no less a tragedy had it happened somewhere else, or to some other child. Part of the heart-wrenching truth was that up until then, despite or maybe because of all the fears and many warnings, no one had been seriously injured in the occupation of Alcatraz. Now a little girl lay dying, and it was Richard's daughter.

In the panicky moments that followed, many rushed to the side of the unconscious child. I think even in those desperate few minutes when people realized how seriously she was hurt there must have been glances among them and questions left unanswered about how it had happened. Yvonne was flown by helicopter to a San Francisco hospital where she died four days later without regaining consciousness. It is well known that Richard immediately demanded a federal investigation into whether she had been pushed off that landing. Witnesses, including at least one of Yvonne's young cousins, were interviewed by federal authorities who concluded that there was no evidence of foul play in the accident. But Richard remained convinced that Yvonne's death could be attributed to his enemies on the island, and Annie, who had feared the island from the beginning, said there had been earlier threats and other violence directed toward her children. All these years later the question of how the fall happened is still debated among those who took part in the Alcatraz occupation.

No matter what actually occurred that January morning, however, the event marked the end of Richard's personal involvement with Alcatraz. In a way it drew a dark shade over the innocence of that first phase of the occupation. Al Miller was of course sitting near his close friend at Yvonne's funeral. It must have seemed that all the others who came to share his grief were at that point vaguely part of the background. "I remember my last conversation with him," Miller said. "He said, 'Well, you guys, do what you can with it. I don't have the heart for it anymore.'"

In a way that I think is telling of what a tragedy it really was, Yvonne's death was felt especially hard by Peter Bowen, the Sausalito sailor who had organized the invasion fleet and had found Yvonne hidden beneath a blanket on his boat that night. "I just couldn't help feeling responsible, somehow, even though they smuggled her on board against my orders," he said. "I had brought her there." At the time Peter was just twenty-five. He had brought many more Indians and supplies to the island after that first night, but after Yvonne died he did not make another trip to Alcatraz.

Federal authorities adopted a stance that was publicly sympathetic to the Oakes family and yet confidentially more perplexed than ever about how to deal with the Indian occupiers. Leonard Garment, President Nixon's White House lawyer, sent Richard and Annie a personal note of condolence, calling the accident "crushing and sorrowful." Tom Hannon, who knew Richard better than any of the other federal representatives and who thought of the young Mohawk almost as a friend, made a personal visit to Richard and Annie.

Behind the public scenes, however, there was dissension among the government officials much as there was among the occupiers. Since the beginning of the occupation, the White House had been flooded with mail about Alcatraz, most of it supporting at least some recognition of the Indians' claims. The U. S. Information Agency had even informed White House staffers that the occupation was receiving much favorable attention overseas. But federal attempts to focus the occupation on some terms that might lead to a settlement had gotten nowhere. Even while Richard had remained the most recognized spokesman for the Indians, the federal authorities could not pin down any clear leadership structure on the island. Early in December they had taken the surplus federal prison off the market for other uses, by including it in the grand creation of the Golden Gate National Recreation Area that swept in a vast stretch of coastal land all the way from Point Reyes in the north to the richly attractive old military properties in Marin County and along the shoreline of the San Francisco peninsula itself. That designation meant almost nothing to the Indians on Alcatraz, however, who vowed they would never under any circumstances share their island as part of a public park. In Washington a team of top agency representatives from the Office of Economic Opportunity, the Department of Labor, the General Services Administration, the FBI, and the office of the vice president was formed to come up with a strategy for Alcatraz. The group was headed by Bob Robertson, the executive director of the National Council on Indian Opportunity, who was considered a friend of the Indian cause.

Others close to the White House were increasingly impatient with the careful approach of Garment and Robertson. Garment's aide, Bradley Patterson, remembers particularly two staffers working directly under White House chief of staff John Ehrlichman, Bud Krogh and Geoff Shepard, who held liason responsibilities between the White House and the FBI and Department of Justice.

"Bud and Geoff saw this as a law enforcement problem," Patterson remembered. "It's a trespass. They were rather willing and anxious to move the Indians off, because they were violating the law. . . . At one point, I remember, one of the staffers called Tom Hannon 'that asshole' who was obstructing their wishes."[1]

For a time, at least, Garment and Patterson could continue to hold off the hawks in the administration, although we learned later that contingency plans were being drawn up as early as January 1970 for a small-scale military raid on the island that would round up and remove all the Indians under the code name Operation Parks. Perhaps the most important thing we didn't know until years later, however, was that we had a secret ally in the Oval Office itself. In his autobiography, Richard Nixon explained that the man he credited with giving him his determination to keep on fighting no matter what the odds was his football coach at Whittier College, a Native American affectionately known as Chief Wallace Newman. "Next to my father," Nixon said, "Chief Newman was the most influential man in my life." I never met Chief Newman, and don't really know anything about him, but I'd like to thank him for the gifts he gave to Richard Nixon. As it turned out they would be of even greater value to our people than Alcatraz alone.

In retrospect I have some sympathy for the frustrations faced by those federal authorities who tried to come up with some deal to end the occupation. I also must admit that some of their methods turned out to be clumsy gestures that probably made things worse. Patterson remembers that among the team in Washington Alcatraz had become a symbolic representation of the problems faced by urban Indians. That would have been a lot closer to correct in October of 1969 than it was early in 1970, when the federal team leader, Bob Robertson, proposed turning over $50,000 in federal poverty money to the Bay Area Native American Council (BANAC). "We wanted to link together the urban Indian organizations in the Bay Area with the militants on Alcatraz," said Patterson.

BANAC had been created specifically to accommodate the government's desire to meet with a representative body of urban Indians. Our United Council in Oakland and the San Francisco Indian Center were not by themselves representative enough to include San Jose and Santa Clara, or the student groups. "Indians of All Tribes," as we had called ourselves at the start of the occupation, didn't meet their needs either. There is a saying: "Get five Indians together and they will form two organizations." BANAC was such a group, with representatives from all the other organizations. But the group on Alcatraz demanded veto power over any decision BANAC made, especially when word spread that the government was offering a $50,000 grant to aid urban Indians.

Unfortunately it was that kind of offer that Al Miller and others on the island saw as an effort to get the mainland to "sell out" the occupiers. The wedge between us was only driven deeper. It was, however, not the government's only offer. In the years since, federal authorities have refused either to confirm or deny it, but Tim Findley says at one point he was used as a go-between to convene a meeting of Alcatraz leaders with Robertson in the posh Marin suburb of Tiburon. In one of the meetings meant to seem like friendly coffee talks, the occupiers were offered control of at least part of Ft. Mason on the San Francisco shoreline in return for giving up their claim to Alcatraz. Ft. Mason occupies one of the most spectacularly scenic spots in the world and might easily be regarded as among the most valuable real estate properties in the United States. The half dozen Alcatraz leaders who came to that secret meeting turned the offer down flat.

With Richard gone, the question of leadership on the island was even more in doubt. Richard may never have taken control, and even Al Miller recalls him as being too much of a "dreamer" to exercise much practical authority.[2] But he was at least recognizable as a figurehead from whom the mood of the occupation might be gauged. In those first cold months of a new year, however, the contest over who would be in charge was taking on an even more rigid and difficult shape.

Stella Leach, biting off her words in a resentful interview with the *San Francisco Chronicle*, said, "You expect us to produce miracles. We've only been here six weeks. You [whites] have had 200 years in dealing with our lives and you've succeeded in dividing us not only by geography, but by your propaganda. . . . What's wrong with Indians now is that no one has ever listened to us. If we can't listen to our own people, then we will end up in the same situation as the BIA. We don't intend to let that happen."

Even so, it was Stella, with her piercing indignation, who had refused to listen to the pan-tribal plans for taking Alcatraz and who, I have always suspected, had something to do with discouraging the boats from showing up for us on November 9. Now, with her own power evident in her position on the seven-member Alcatraz Council (and that of her son David as well), Stella at least talked a line of democratic decision making. The truth of the matter was a lot less welcoming.

Al Miller is only one of many Alcatraz veterans who recall the influence of drugs and violence on the island during that period. "This gang leader, and this lady that was really helpful to them, running the clinic, and she had kind of put an idea in their heads that they should run the island," he remembered. The Thunderbirds of Oakland already had some experience with drug dealing. They were streetwise and tough, and at least one resident of the island at the time remembers that they were inclined to swing chains as one of their weapons. The big weapon, though, was drugs. I don't want to believe that Stella, a nurse who had developed highly respectable credentials in working with children, would have had anything to do with bringing narcotics on to the island. But others have said that she at least turned her head when those associated with her sons brought out marijuana and even heroin.

We on the mainland knew only the rumors. Our attempts with Vine and others to bring back some greater sense of purpose had been met with threats. I recall being in the Indian Center one day when a young woman I barely knew approached me and said, "I'm surprised you're still here. They told me they were going to throw you in the Bay."

I wasn't an old man then, and I've never been a coward, but I'm not a fool either. Others felt as I did, realizing that further attempts to step into the chaos of leadership on the island were not only futile but dangerous. It was at this point that I think John Trudell and, to a certain extent, La Nada, deserve most credit for preserving our respect on the island.

John was a Navy veteran in his second year of studying for a degree in broadcasting at a small college in San Bernardino, California. He had first heard of the invasion from friends at UCLA, but it was not until Thanksgiving that he hitchhiked up the coast for his first visit to Alcatraz. In that celebration and from a meeting he had with Richard, John was convinced that Alcatraz was the path back to his Santee Sioux roots. Before Christmas he moved his family to the island. In the same way familiar to many, he found himself involved first in the roughly organized security detail. He had a certain charisma that drew others to him as a spokesman, and it was John whom Jerry Hill and his friend, Rock, first asked to represent their concerns over organization.

John's experience with broadcasting proved to be his greatest advantage. The Berkeley-based radio station KPFA was by then already established as a landmark of public broadcasting from a perspective well to the left of any commercial stations. When KPFA offered to set up a transmitter link to the island for regular daily reports, John was the natural choice as the island's spokesman. I don't think there is any doubt that by then the occupation had become far more politicized and radical than when I produced the first Proclamation early in November. The occupiers needed to find a new expression that would assert their determination and even counter the media doubt that had arisen since the publication of Findley's stories. John could convey the message with a smooth delivery that soon extended from Berkeley to radio links as far away as New York City. Even so, the ideas and the more-structured demands for money to create a permanent Native American university on the island had to come from someone with more direct experience. That job, and really that direction in leadership, went to

John Trudell. Photograph by Ilka Hartmann.

La Nada. Much of it may have been a re-expression from the angry intellectual approach encouraged by Lee Brightman at Berkeley, but in important ways it served to provide some new definition to what had begun to veer wildly into anarchy. In the next few months LaNada and John had the principle roles in the most difficult time of all on Indian Alcatraz.

■

Jerry Hill stayed on until almost the start of summer. To him the experience was a great journey of both pride and misery, but a path toward spiritual and intellectual enlightenment. However much it must be honestly said that there was trouble on the island, that greater sense of learning and growing together is still what is remembered most by everyone who had the experience. Divisions and disputes there certainly were, but an entirely new sense of Native American unity was the real reward.

Jerry had made one of his periodic mind-clearing trips back to the mainland that late spring, 1970. He was at Fisherman's Wharf waiting for the last evening boat to return to the island. "There was a bunch of drunk guys who were there, and they were talking about killing somebody. I didn't know if they were talking drunk, or if it was real or not real. I just had this moral conflict with myself about what I could do to stop it or interfere in some way, or whether it was anything real at all."

The boat pulled up in the dimming light, and Jerry watched the young men board ahead of him.

"I just stepped away and said 'I'm not going,' and somebody jumped up and took my place. Then I stood there and watched the boat leave. I felt cowardly almost, but I just said to myself, 'I can't do this.'"

19

The Feds, the Fire

IF INDIAN PEOPLE OF ALL TRIBES share one thing in their heritage, it's that they have no reason for putting their trust in the U.S. government. It doesn't really matter whether the politics of the time happen to be more liberal and inclined toward civil rights or whether they tilt the other way in putting property over people. Indians can vote (though most of them don't), and they can lobby for the good causes and the good candidates just like anybody else. But they can't hand over their heritage and their freedom to an authority that is by definition their natural enemy. Even the government understands this. No matter how generous the political leaders may sound, part of the function of the federal government has always been to make sure Indians stay in their place as captive cultures. Alcatraz suggested they might be breaking out and coalescing into something else that was subversive by definition.

The occupation of the island was immensely inspiring to Indians and to many non-Indians alike for its demonstration of the rise of Native American consciousness and activism. But meaning and actual purpose are not one and the same. In that dark part of the federal government where purpose is always regarded with suspicion, the uncertainty over what the Indians really intended to do with the Rock led to all sorts of unfriendly ideas.

Years after the occupation I acquired a copy of my own FBI file under terms of the Freedom of Information Act. Like most of those documents, a lot of it was blacked out and unreadable, but the part that was left in was a real eye opener. It included an urgent teletype to FBI offices all over the country from the acting director, concerning "Adam Nordwall, EM–AIM. Subject reportedly president of American Indian Movement (AIM) San Leandro, California, and organizer in Alcatraz Prison takeover. Partial Chippewa Indian from the Red Leg Reservation in Red Leg, Minnesota."

It included a note from the Domestic Intelligence Division, alerting the recipients:

All offices having Indian reservation communities or groups in their territory, according to Bureau of Indian Affairs official publication, being instructed to alert sources, local and Federal authorities and to be alert for any violation of Federal or local statutes. We are maintaining contact with source and conducting investigation to further identify Nordwall.
    Copy of attached being furnished to Internal Security and Criminal Divisions of the Department, Secret Service, and Department of Interior."

Attached was a formal notification from Acting FBI Director L. Patrick Gray III, marking me down as "potentially dangerous because of background, emotional instability or activity in groups engaged in activities inimical to U.S."

Aside from the fact that there is no such place as Red Leg, Minnesota, anywhere near my own home reservation of Red Lake, and the fact that AIM not only never organized in the sleepy suburb of San Leandro but actually took me and my role to be too "establishment" for their cause, I think I would have to concede to "activities inimical to U.S." Like other Indians, I was born that way.

On Alcatraz there was always an awareness that somebody might be an "agent." If for no other reason, that was just a part of the general paranoia at the time. On the mainland I was surprised to find one young woman working daily in the support group office who said she was able to do so because she had been given time off from her official obligations to the U.S. Army.

Brooks Townes, the crewman aboard the *Seaweed* who landed with the first invaders on November 20 and who spent nine days himself on the island, was surprised to run into a Sausalito neighbor years later who showed him aerial photographs of Indians in the lower yard waving happily to the low-passing plane. Brooks's neighbor explained that he had been hired to take the pictures by agents of the army's Special Forces.

Even Tim Findley and *Chronicle* photographer Vince Maggiora always assumed that Maggiora's exclusive pictures taken the night of the November 20 landing were never published because the timing didn't match with the morning paper's deadline. It was more than twenty-five years later that they learned that FBI agents had approached the executive editor of the paper demanding to examine Maggiora's negatives and threatening to produce a subpoena if the editor refused. The editor says he told the agents he had destroyed the negatives rather than turn them over. Some of those pictures are published for the first time in this book. They show one of the boats and many of the invaders, obviously what the FBI wanted to examine.

It was *Chronicle* columnist Herb Caen who revealed the secret details of a planned counterinvasion by an armed force of military and federal marshals. The special unit was to be trained and staged from Angel Island in the Bay under the code name "Operation Parks." Caen blew their cover and the action never happened, but the government did not deny they had such plans.

I don't know if there were ever federal agents planted among the occupiers or among those of us in the mainland support group. I assume, however, that at some point there must have been. By all indications, the invasion itself was carried off with as much of a surprise to have included an agent who was aware of all the planning. But later events have always raised disturbing questions about how much the government may have involved itself in a secret attempt to sabotage the occupation.

At least for those very difficult times at the beginning of 1970, however, the continued chaotic condition of leadership and control on the island did its own part to undermine earlier support. Sadly, I think, it was those eccentric skippers and sailors from the Sausalito Navy who were among the first to give up on what had been their continual and generous support. Mary Crowley, the eighteen-year-old whiz kid who had daringly brought out some of the first invaders under sail in the darkness, said she remembers it still as "one of the truly great experiences of my life." She carried out boatloads of people young and old for days afterward, meeting "wonderful people. People who told me it was the first time in their lives that they felt really proud to be an Indian." So inspired was Mary by it all that at first she dedicated her time not only to bringing more people and supplies by boat, but to convincing others she knew to offer their support. It had been Mary, we learned later, who first talked the Bratskeller (along with Perry's and Victoria Station) to contribute all that food for the first Thanksgiving on the island. By January there were so many other people supporting the occupiers that Mary felt it was now time to go back to the other parts of her life.

Brooks Townes had lived on the island for nine days. He gave up returning to it after a dispute with a young Indian he didn't know over whether there was room on the boat for three Indians or for a television crew from NBC. Brooks finally conceded to taking the Indians out first and returning for the television crew, but when he met the young Indian on the dock later, their exchange of angry words led to both of them pulling out knives. Al Miller stepped between them and no one was hurt, but an important bit of support from the North Bay was lost.

It was true that the occupiers had increasingly established their independence from reliance on outside help. The rock group Creedence Clearwater had provided a donation which made it possible for the occupiers to purchase their own multipassenger fishing boat and rename it the *Clearwater*. Donations still came into the bank account set up by Dorothy Miller at the Bank of California, although the withdrawals frequently seemed more intended for nights on the mainland than for supplies to the island.

Bob Robertson's idea on behalf of the government was to incorporate Alcatraz as part of the newly designated Golden Gate National Recreation Area, but to reserve it as a park with an Indian theme dedicated to the pride of Native Americans. Such a proposal obviously had no chance of success with the occupiers, especially if it provided for no control by Indians themselves of the island or its visitors. What the occupiers, Indians of All Tribes, demanded was a minimum $300,000 planning grant from the government to establish a Native American cultural and spiritual center on the island.

Early in April the council on the island called a news conference to be held in the lower yard at which they would explain their demands. Media men and women who showed up at Fisherman's Wharf to board one of the two boats the Indians would permit to land on the island were charged $10 each before they could take the short ride out to cover the news conference. It got the predictable coverage in their accounts, and one more crucial link of support by the media was cut.

The mood among the press was growing increasingly impatient with the hostile stance of the occupiers and the continued indecisiveness of the federal authorities. Another critical moment was at hand.

In response to the occupiers' rejection of the park proposal, the government cut off all supplies of water and power to the island. This was the same threat with which Tom Hannon had tried to bluff Richard on the first day, but this time both the government and the occupiers were better prepared. There was still plenty of support left and even vessels available to be certain that water could be brought to the island. Gasoline-powered generators had been used for varying purposes since the beginning. The most obvious loss would be in cutting off the power supplying the Alcatraz lighthouse, which had continued its steady reliable sweep of the Bay to alert mariners of the obstacle. In the interim the Coast Guard had installed new anchored buoys with their own beacons and electronic signals that made the old lighthouse obsolete. It went dark, leaving the island at night as if surrounded by a noose of floating buoys.

That was the government's mistake. The lighthouse meant more to the view-conscious establishment of San Francisco than just a means of preventing collisions with the Rock. The rotating beacon was part of history, like a touchstone on which to identify this spectacular setting and its richly colorful past. No way were they going to accept it being blotted out as part of the game of attrition with the Indians. Their bottom line was that they didn't really care about who "owned" the island so long as that lighthouse kept working, and the only way to make sure of that was to deal directly with the Indians themselves. As it turned out, both sides—the occupiers and the federal government—missed their best chances at winning.

On the night of June 1, 1970, as the fingers of summer fog stretched in their annual reach into the Bay, at least one fire, more likely two or more that were simultaneously burning, broke out on Alcatraz.

La Nada remembers that she and John Trudell were on the mainland doing a radio broadcast. Others have said they thought Trudell was broadcasting directly from the island as the fires raged. Jerry Hill, perhaps as telling in his description as any, recalls that it all seemed to have happened within the general haze of dream-laden smoke from the night's passing joints.

It caused a weird yellow-orange luminescence on the Bay as the color of the flames was diffused by the thick fog. Shortly before 11:00 P.M. the Coast Guard dispatched a boat from Oakland to investigate the strange glow. Within twenty minutes the reports back to the mainland were that the entire east side of the island was in flames.

It is still unclear how many people were actually on Alcatraz that night, but earlier there had been meetings discussing what to do about the removal of the water barge. The blaze, centered at the top of the hill in the faded stateliness of the warden's house, was too far to be reached from the shoreline by the fireboat from San Francisco, and in any case Indians along the dock were warning away the Coast Guard and other boats, shouting back that everyone was safe, no one was in need of rescue. The fire raged without anything but the damp fog to slow its destructive course.

"We tried to keep the lighthouse from going, but it went, and there was nothing we could do about it," Trudell reported in his radio broadcast the next night. "We didn't have any water to fight it with, and by the time the Coast Guard came, it was too late for them to do anything, so we didn't let them come on the island. . . . We didn't know if they were going to try to take us off the island, or what, and we didn't want all of those government people running around at night, so we just kept them off. . . . We made an attempt to stop the lighthouse fire. We couldn't do that, so we just let it all go."

However it had begun—some claimed from a flare fired by a passing boat, others suggested secret agents, and most suspected the Indians themselves—the fire was an expression that needed no analysis of how far things had gotten out of hand on the island. Almost immediately there were calls in the media for federal authorities to bring some end to the occupation.

But twice in his radio report Trudell had stressed that the occupiers had made an attempt to halt the fire from spreading to the lighthouse. It was, he already knew, the one spot on the island that the most important powers in San Francisco really cared about.

Tim Findley had taken himself off all Alcatraz coverage after producing his own critical pieces about the leadership struggles. He was not expecting to be called to the waterfront high rise where the *Chronicle*'s editor-in-chief, Scott Newhall, held a personal domain over his beloved Bay. Newhall said he had already made arrangements to supply a powerful new generator to the Indians on the island. The tradeoff was to be that they keep the lighthouse going, but the fire had made that even more problematic, and the attitudes of the Indians on the island, he said, couldn't be trusted. He wanted somebody who knew them to quietly take care of the details.

Findley was not being assigned a story for the paper. Newhall did not want the *Chronicle*'s participation known in any way. But part of the problem was that the fire had damaged the key bulb in the lighthouse. It would have to be replaced, and since the Coast Guard could not be a source, Newhall had found a theatrical supply house that would supply the bulb. It would be installed by the newspaper's chief electrician, but he would need an escort to get past the Indians. It was, Findley said, the very last card he thought he had left in dealing with Alcatraz, but he managed to arrange with La Nada a trip to the island with the electrician and the bulb.

On the way out he stood on the deck next to her, not knowing quite what to say to the former friend and compatriot in the cause. "They told me I should throw you off the boat on the way out here," she said at last, looking at him with an expression that suggested she was still thinking about committing such a betrayal.

The lighthouse was rekindled on June 4. The *Chronicle* ran a front page story by another reporter, never mentioning the paper's own role in making it possible. The story quoted John Trudell: "For us on the island, and for Indians everywhere, it is a symbol of the rekindled hope that some day the just claims and rightful dignity of the American Indians will be recognized by our fellow citizens. . . . It was in peaceful search of this recognition that we came to the island last November. . . . As long as the light glows, the search will go on."

20

Siege

So it went on through what I call the third phase of the Alcatraz occupation. There was no longer that idealistic enthusiasm of the young students in the first group. Nor would the gangster attitude brought from the streets prevail for long. Parts of both remained on the island, carrying out their separate visions of what would become of it. La Nada stayed almost to the very end and would endure yet another fire on the island in which her hands were seriously burned in a desperate attempt to beat back the flames threatening her son. The greedy ones who saw some profit to be gained for themselves continued to come and go with their own intentions, so much so that eventually three young Indian men faced charges from accumulated evidence of their theft of copper wire and other salvageable materials—total value $600. Nevertheless, Alcatraz and its meaning were not to be defined from that point on by the few Indians who continued to try to live there. John Trudell, acknowledged as the island spokesman but never afforded the same romanticized image as Richard had experienced, conceded in his interviews that the island could not sustain a large occupation for long.

"At times, the outside would look at it and say, 'well, you're having fights out there' or 'there's internal dissension,' or this and that. But they weren't being practical. You can't keep four hundred people there unless you lock them in the cells the way the government did. . . . In the end, it had to do with what the island can support, especially after they shut off our water and they shut the electricity down. There were just certain things that were. . . . It's actually that we were literally back on the reservation."[1]

The big fire in June had only made the island even more uninhabitable. The old warden's house, which had offered the first warm refuge of the invasion, was a gutted shell, visible from all around the Bay as a hollow monument to the lack of leadership. There were still warm apartments and

representing some ten thousand Indians in California. Only a year earlier I had chased a federal panel from San Francisco to Sacramento to Fresno just to get a few minutes' hearing. Now the BIA itself was admitting that California tribes should be better represented in deciding the future of some half a million acres controlled by the tribes in the state. In Nevada, Paiutes at Pyramid Lake took their first steps to win back legal control of the Truckee River from farmers diverting the river to irrigation.

All this was news, frequently found on the front pages of the major papers. On the inside pages, where Native Americans had seldom before been portrayed as more than cartoon characters, new stories began to appear, stories that probed the reasons for the high rate of suicide among Indians on the reservations and the equally shocking rate of infant mortality. Poverty and unemployment were beginning to be reported not just as characteristic of reservation life, but as the result of efforts made by the dominant white society itself to destroy Indian cultures. Alcatraz, it could be said, brought attention to the cause, but it was also bringing back pride.

That, I suppose, is what Richard felt, too. We had not stayed in touch with each other after Richard and the others on the island proclaimed themselves to be distinctly apart from those of us on the mainland. As all Indian people had done, we shared in Richard and Annie's grief when Yvonne was killed. We had asked a great deal from that one family, and they sacrificed far more than we ever intended. For my part, and for that of most of us on the mainland, the efforts after that had been to find some way to bring everyone together again. I put forward the idea to the occupiers that at least we should make use of all the curiosity about the island and even renew and expand some goodwill by offering guided tours of the cell block. "We're not monkeys in a zoo," I was told. "We don't want people coming out here to look at us." Even so, the island leadership in June tried to start twice-a-day tours at $5 per person. The plan was stopped when the Coast Guard threatened to lift the permits of boat owners involved. After the removal of the water barge and the subsequent fire, federal authorities began reporting that sewage was backing up on the island, posing even more of a health hazard. I remember showing newspaper accounts to Cy Williams in which Tom Hannon was reported as saying that Alcatraz had become nothing more than "an island ghetto."

Cy, in his usual brusque way, tossed the paper aside. "First they took away the water barge so the toilets couldn't flush," he said. "Then they pulled the electrical power, turned up the heat with fires, and now they're trying to bury us with bullshit." Only Cy was sort of mad at everybody, not just the federal government. Among those of us who were not old but "older," there was a sense of helplessness about what might happen next.

I cannot say that he confided in me about it, but I was told by others, and it does seem obvious from his actions, that at least part of Richard's ambition in those difficult months during the spring of 1970 was to develop a following strong enough for him to recapture control of the island and its meaning. I doubt seriously if he would have told Annie this, knowing her fears from the start and her agony over the loss of her daughter. Perhaps Richard in his own way did not admit it to himself, but what he seemed to be looking for was the restoration of the image that had been made of him. Sadly, I almost think of it in terms of people asking, "What ever happened to Victor Mature?"

In addition to advising the Pit River protestors, Richard had led a sit-in protest in March at the Alameda headquarters of the Bureau of Indian Affairs, demanding the dismissal of Commissioner Louis Bruce. He and twelve others were arrested.

In a way that is perhaps telling of something else, Richard remained closer to *Chronicle* reporter Tim Findley than to me in those days. In asking for her memories years later, Tim's wife at the time, Marilyn, said her strongest recollection was of Annie and Richard coming to dinner at their house after Yvonne's death, and of Richard being too busily involved in discussing his new plans to notice his other children playing too close to the edge of the deck on Findley's steep hillside home. "It was just chilling somehow," she said.

And maybe that tells us something. Maybe the reputation Richard enjoyed as a high steel worker, correct or not, itself fits with how close to the edge he always seemed to play it. On the night of June 11, 1970, he told Annie he was going back to Warren's for a while in an effort to mend some fences among his old friends at the Little Res. In one way, at least, it had been Warren's where it had all started. The fire that previous October that had destroyed the San Francisco Indian Center had long been considered to be the result of a turf war in the neighborhood between Indians and Samoans, much of it starting from conflicts begun at Warren's Bar. Richard had been the bartender there when he first came to the city, and later he had patrolled the streets with Al Miller in an effort to reduce the tensions. Many of the first young people to invade Alcatraz had been recruited out of the bar. But that night something in the way Richard approached his old home ground was tragically wrong. A fight broke out around the pool tables. Richard, either in the thick of it or trying to stop it, was struck and floored by the blunt end of a pool cue. Witnesses said that after he went down he was hit again in the back of the head. They identified his assailant as a young Samoan.

Friends of Richard's—I'm not sure who—carried him unconscious out to a car and back to his apartment at San Francisco State's "Gatorville" married student housing complex. They told Annie he was merely drunk. It was not until the next morning when she was unable to waken him that Annie called for an ambulance. Doctors who examined him said his skull was fractured and immediately took him into surgery. He remained in a coma for an entire month.

Ten days after receiving him at the hospital, doctors at San Francisco General held little hope that Richard would ever regain consciousness, let alone recover from the effects of the beating. With Annie constantly at his side, and nothing more they could do except to sustain his life functions, the doctors permitted three medicine men to attend the critically injured Mohawk with treatments of prayers and specially prepared herbs. Mad Bear Anderson, the Tuscarora medicine man, came all the way from Niagara Falls, New York. Peter Mitten came from Ontario, Canada, and Thomas Banyacya from the Hopi Reservation in Arizona. The hospital doctors made patient, understanding noises, but obviously did not believe it when the medicine men said Richard was getting better.

It was noted as being against medical advice when Richard checked himself out of scheduled therapy some three weeks later and returned home. He was no longer the ruggedly handsome and powerful young man who had twice dived into the Bay and swum to Alcatraz. His head had been shaved for the surgery, and there was a twist of paralysis all along his left side that slowed his movements and slurred his speech. As with all people so terribly injured, there seemed something uncertain in his eyes about whether all the memories would ever return. A blaze was still burning in his spirit, however, as he credited the medicine men alone for his recovery.

On the island they conducted their own less traditional services for Richard's recovery, aware of their politically agnostic stance in the continuing siege and of the contradictions still lingering over the struggle for leadership. Despite the *Chronicle*'s efforts, the lighthouse was never repaired to be a reliable beacon as had been hoped. Fuel to keep the generator running was increasingly a problem, and many on the island saw no need to continue tending to the chore of keeping it going. The Coast Guard was receiving more complaints from what they described as "mariners," but were as likely to be preservationists demanding that permanent power be restored to the lighthouse. John Trudell, at last holding a good card that could be played wisely, told the Coast Guard and Tom Hannon that the occupiers would not permit permanent restoration of power to the lighthouse unless electricity was restored to other parts of the island and the water barge returned. Hannon, caught more and more in the middle of the unseen power struggle in Washington, replied that it was "not in my power to provide services to anyone other than government employees." In a way, I guess you could say Hannon was nearly as beat up as Richard.

In Washington, San Francisco's most powerful politician, Congressman Phillip Burton, a Democrat, offered a bill that proposed to settle the whole thing by selling the island to the Indians for $24.00. It is in Burton's memory today that the entire vast expanse of the Golden Gate National Recreation Area is remembered as his finest personal and political achievement. It is not remembered at all, however, that eliminated from the bill creating that huge public park was a provision to sell Alcatraz back to the Indians for the same price paid by whites for Manhattan Island. That was exactly what I had proposed to the San Francisco Board of Supervisors just one year earlier.

That August, the *Harbor Queen*, one of the tour boats making ever more daring passes closer and closer to Alcatraz, paddled along the eastern lee side of the island with a guide chatting away about the sinister past of convicts held there and the strange condition of Indians now holding out there. As the tourists leaned against the rail and aimed their lenses in the direction of the Rock, a loud "whanging" sound suddenly was heard on the upper metal bulkhead. The *Harbor Queen* had been struck broadside by an arrow obviously fired from Alcatraz. To some it was the equivalent of the mysterious Vietnamese torpedo attack in the Gulf of Tonkin, with just such implications of war.

It was absurd, of course, but the arrow that struck the *Harbor Queen* was the incident that many had been waiting for to establish that the Indians on Alcatraz were some kind of threat to innocent Americans. Some indignant people huffed and puffed about it being reason enough to remove them at once. John Trudell, obviously learning as he went along, replied that the occupiers had asked the tour boats to stay clear and then had asked the Coast Guard to make sure that they did, all to no avail. Running close alongside the island peering and pointing at the Indians was a disrespectful act anyone would want stopped, he pointed out. "And now, with one 42-cent arrow, we've stopped it," he said.

As I said at the beginning, this story is, like all life's stories, a circle. Perhaps before I reach the end you will begin to see it closing.

In September, some two weeks after he had checked himself out of the hospital, Richard Oakes told the *Chronicle* he was setting out on a new adventure. With Annie and the kids and three others, including two white men to help, Richard planned to leave in a battered old school bus he called his "traveling college" on a tour of reservations and Indian communities all over the country. He would acquire knowledge along the way, he said, and pass on his own experiences in a continuously mobile search for spirituality and what he called "the basic factor of 'Indian-ness.'"

He was almost exactly restating of what he had first heard from the visiting White Roots of Peace soon after he had come to San Francisco State. "We will go and learn wherever we can, and maybe the result will be that we will return with not just one bus, but with a caravan—an army—of Indian people to reclaim their history and their land with new pride."

In addition to the donated old bus, Richard had $300 to begin his journey. He was counting, he said, on getting more support from reservations along the way. "After all, it's been a hell of a year. But I think I have to get a positive response out of nature sometime, and I think this time I'll find it."

"It is a time of slogans," he said, still struggling with his words. "White is right. Black is beautiful. I plan to add one more: Indians are permanent."

21

Thunderbird U

THROUGH THE SUMMER MONTHS and into the early fall, the character and size of the occupation fluctuated with the students coming from and going to their classes. It never again reached the level of active and continuously creative involvement that we had seen at the beginning, but the renewed presence of Indian students making pilgrimages of perhaps only a day or two at a time offset what had become the hard edge imposed by less-directed street people who had taken up residence on the island.

La Nada and John Trudell (the spokesman of words often written by her) never gave up on the concept of creating a stable Native American university on the island. Her proposals for it even included a name that indirectly gave credence to the biker group of which her brother was a member. It was to be called "Thunderbird University." Federal authorities, of course, had no intention of supporting any such proposal but they did, up to a point, listen. That point was reached, I think, at one of the many mainland meetings Bob Robertson convened in an attempt to convince the occupiers to accept some piece of the new park in exchange for leaving Alcatraz. One of Robertson's aides insisted he saw David Leach, Stella's son, drop a small tablet into a cup of coffee later put in front of the federal team leader. Robertson was warned not to drink it. So far as I know it was never analyzed. The tablet may only have been saccharin, but there were rumors among the Indians, and the feds believed them, that it was actually mescaline.

We didn't need to drug the federal government, and it wouldn't have worked anyway. I think now, as I look back on it, that part of our problem was the inability to recognize how successful we had been in dazzling the U.S. authorities. We had the attention of the White House beyond even what we had imagined. La Nada and others had been to Washington, D.C., to carry on part of the discussions. Secrets about training a special force just to deal with the occupiers had been leaked. There was a whole team assembled in part from White House staffers assigned to virtually nothing else but reaching some solution to the occupation. Yet we didn't quite see it. Internal memos in the office of the president compared the delicacy of reaching some settlement with us to the risks involved in creating another Kent State, where four students had been shot and killed during an antiwar protest. There were even comparisons to the public outrage over the My Lai massacre in Vietnam revealed that year. As long as we held Alcatraz we occupied a pivotal point in the balance of political power in America. But we didn't quite see it that way.

In 1970 Indians, the forgotten people of only a year before, suddenly seemed to be everywhere. I also remember the personal frustrations and the true tragedies that came from the soured struggle over leadership and direction on Indian Alcatraz. But I am absolutely certain that those things were petty and ultimately meaningless in contrast to the historic impact that the island has had for our people.

■

Before it was over, by the way, that $16,000 from Tom Mudd that had so divided us over its use had been employed to support eighty young Native Americans returning to college. I mark that as one of my proudest achievements. It was true that we on the mainland and in BANAC were regarded with grim suspicion by the increasingly isolated leadership on the island. But we did not transfer that into any public bickering or disputes that might lessen the sense of unity in the emerging movement. Don Patterson, I know, began to feel some despair over the indifference to what had been part of the objective in the first place—the reconstruction of the burned-out San Francisco Indian Center. The center still operated out of the temporary storefront but was now almost totally devoted to the logistical support of Alcatraz. "We've been forgotten, Adam," he told me. "And when it's over, it may be even harder to find the money."

BANAC had seen fractures emerge and deepen in its membership, particularly during Stella's attempt to dominate the island. Mistrust over the management of small sums of money or minor unintentional slights at weekend powwows seemed to be exaggerated by the implied political contest between traditional leadership and Alcatraz militancy. I occupied a place that I thought should have been somewhere reasonably in the center of it all, between my instigation of the invasion and my appeals to make better use of it, but sometimes it is in the center of a circle where all the shots get mistakenly aimed.

No different than Richard, maybe, I felt a need to restore my own sense of leadership. The Italians, after all, were still intending to carry on with their annual charade of "discovery" that Columbus Day in the San Francisco Marina. Busy with our own plans for invasion, we had left them alone since the "scalping" incident in 1968, but by the turn of a new decade I thought it was time to renew our interest. Besides, at that point we needed a little light diversion.

Joe Cervetto, the city's annual Columbus, was interviewed before the event and spoke proudly about his new $595 costume made especially in Genoa, Italy, for the occasion. He added boldly, and with some defiance, that "This year I won't be wearing any hat. Only the toupee." Well, what would you do?

Cy and Meade Chibetty, and I and our families, along with many others from the United Council, donned our traditional outfits and headed across the Bay Bridge on the familiar route to the San Francisco Marina. We made our camp on the lawn, a discreet distance down the beach from where Cervetto was to make his annual landing. Actually, my intention—the intention of all of us—was to make amends with the friendly Italian businessman. I brought along a pipe that I intended to present and smoke with him as a gesture of peace since our last encounter.

"Sure you will, oh sure," Cy muttered, as he saw the police van pulling up behind the bleachers between us and the beachfront landing spot. Cervetto, I'm positive, must have noticed us as the little rowboat took him to shore in this newly staged re-enactment, but he carried on with the customary stab in the sand as if bravely oblivious of our little crowd of Indians who now started walking up the beach with me and my pipe at their head. We had gotten no closer than fifty yards when the riot cops with their long heavy sticks formed a blank blue line in front of us.

"Now what, leader?" Meade Chibetty whispered in my ear, as I marched up to meet the uniformed police lieutenant nose-to-nose. "That's far enough," the cop told me. "It's only official Columbus Day participants from here on." Cy started laughing.

■

Was some of it competition? A contest among us to establish a warrior's place in counting many coups? Well, probably. But that didn't diminish the fact that Alcatraz inspired involvement in a way beyond any single action of Native Americans since the massacre at Wounded Knee in 1890.

As you may recall, it was Lehman Brightman of UC–Berkeley who mocked our earliest efforts to seize the island as "clownish." In 1970, though, Lehman put himself at the head of such public actions, first to protest the killing of a young Hoopa boy in Sacramento, and later at Mt. Rushmore in the Black Hills, where he and others formed a campground demanding recognition of Sioux rights under the 1868 treaty and the return of more than 100,000 acres taken by the government for a gunnery range.

In the first week of November in that year, at least twenty-five Indians, including Grace Thorpe (who was still officially the public relations person for Alcatraz), scaled a chainlink fence and occupied a former army communications center near the campus of the University of California at Davis. The surplus 640-acre site was about to be turned over to UC–Davis for use as a primate research center and for the study of rice production in the state. The combined force of Indians and Hispanics who set up their occupation demanded it be turned over to them as a center for ethnic studies to be known as Daganawidah-Quetzalcoatl University (DQU). The federal government and UC–Davis agreed to the demands with remarkably little resistance, and DQU became a crowning accomplishment in our attempts to secure facilities devoted to studies of our own cultures. The university was established through the work of David Risling, Jr., and Jack Forbes, both of them cautious academics who had doubted the actions at Alcatraz. In that same week in November 1970, three other surplus military sites in California were occupied by Indians, though with less positive results.

At Ft. Lawton, Washington, a similar protest begun earlier was about to secure that abandoned base as a spiritual and cultural center for people of the Northwest. There were occupations on an island in upstate New York and at a lighthouse in Michigan, and even an attempt to invade Ellis Island in Manhattan Harbor that was only foiled by the familiar problem of unreliable boats. In every case the media cited the participation of "Alcatraz veterans" or the inspiration of the Alcatraz occupation.

In 1970, we were approaching the first anniversary of the Alcatraz invasion with plenty to crow about in terms of how much better the entire world understood the cause of Native Americans and their legitimate claim to restoration of their lands and their cultures. Yet the historical and cultural differences within our group had not melted away. In some ways, perhaps, the experience of Alcatraz had made them even more obvious. It would always trouble me, for example, that Lee Brightman and others who followed his way tried to make our earliest efforts seem less than serious. To Brightman, who for as long as I had known him had presented himself in a buzz haircut and physically imposing stature, our presence in traditional and dance regalia was somehow "clownish." That characterization I will never accept, and the issue of dress itself raises some serious questions about racism in America. Wherever we had gone in the early sixties, whether it was to San Quentin prison or to a U.S. Senate hearing, we had worn at least part of our traditional dress. It was never a costume. It was, in fact, a way of declaring our culture. We wore our "Indian-ness" as a statement of who we were and as a reminder of what had been taken from us. I believe our way of presenting ourselves helped a lot of non-Indians recognize the justice of our cause. If it made some of them feel guilty, then I think their feelings were appropriate. If it made others feel proud, then I think it was also appropriate. But younger people, especially those more politicized by the times, didn't carry their culture on their backs in the same way. In dashes of color or bands of beads, their expression was more contemporary in some ways but also more adjusted to fit with the trend toward identification that identified them with other ethnic groups as well. Sometimes, I think, they felt privately embarrassed by elders in more traditional dress. To them it was the rage and frustration of reality that needed to be expressed, not the claim of culture. There was a great difference between the head-down charge of Lehman Brightman with his crew cut and my own dancing way with a porcupine roach on my head. Both ways were right, especially in those times. Yet the distinction between "traditionals" and contemporary Native Americans is still not easy to understand, even for Indians. We had an advantage in who we were in the late sixties, and sometimes even in what we wore, but real progress and real unity among us would require more than just a shallow judgment of fashion. However much we might gain colorful headlines in places where Indians were still curiosities, the practical conditions of discrimination and racism remained the reality in all our lives.

It was a telling description of the differences that had grown between us that two commemorations of that first anniversary of the Alcatraz invasion were held. The one I led for those of us on the mainland was, of course, closer to the November 9, 1969, date of the first landing. We invited the whole city and anybody to join us for a memorial powwow in the sylvan glens of San Francisco's Stern Grove, an especially dignified bit of preserved wilderness known for its poetry readings and concerts. More than a thousand people showed up for the event. It was then that I announced we intended the following day to correct a four-hundred-year-old error by reclaiming the San Francisco waterfront from the descendants of Sir Francis Drake. I couldn't help noticing that although the press in attendance was skeptical as usual, it was clearly not inclined to ignore me as easily as they had a year or two earlier.

We did indeed return to the Port of San Francisco the following day, outfitted as usual in our traditional finest. We went directly to where builders were intending to dig a new hole along the waterfront for the U.S. Steel skyscraper, a controversial project of its time. I suppose there was some apprehension among the media as I searched around and finally found a manhole cover in which to stab my ceremonial spear. Now what? But I was feeling generous that day, and besides that we really hadn't brought along anybody more militant than Cy with whom to start an occupation. So I looked around the crowd and finally selected someone to carry on. It is duly reported and recorded that Carol Simpson, a shy twenty-three-year-old telephone company worker on her lunch break, accepted the "deed" of eagle feathers I gave her that day as the trustee of our newly reclaimed waterfront. I even gave her the same beaded headband I had loaned Richard on November 9, 1969. If you have a problem with the Port of San Francisco today, I suggest you look up Carol Simpson. I gave it to her. The U.S. Steel high-rise, by the way, was never built.

The commemoration of that first anniversary was, of course, a much more serious affair on Alcatraz itself. La Nada and John Trudell called a news conference at which they and some ninety others (who claimed they were continuing the occupation) presented their plans for future development of the island. They featured an impressive model of a kind of large ceremonial roundhouse surrounded by ninety-six other circular buildings intended to be residences for three hundred students attending the free university, Thunderbird U. The plan, created by the San Francisco architectural firm of Donald McDonald, estimated the cost of a such a renovation at around $6 million. John and La Nada were vague about where that money might come from, but La Nada suggested part of it might be found from selling on the island Native American art and craft work from all over the country.

If some of us might have shaken our heads over how unrealistic and even hopeless those plans sounded, perhaps part of the reason was that we had not taken stock of how far dreams and pure creative energy had already taken us. For neither the news conference on Alcatraz nor our celebrations on the mainland paid much attention to what was already the most stunning and historic victory of all.

■

On July 8, 1970, President Richard Nixon went before the Congress of the United States and publicly denounced "centuries of injustice" to American Indian people that he said amounted to a history of white "aggression, broken agreements, intermittent remorse and prolonged failure" in dealings with people native to this continent.[1]

In the most dramatic reversal in the history of U.S. policy toward Indians, Nixon formally renounced and ended the policy of Termination of tribes and said he was sending to Congress a bill that would give tribal governments authority over existing programs affecting Native Americans. On that same day he announced his support of a House resolution that would return Blue Lake and forty-eight thousand acres to the Taos Pueblos.[2] Within the days and weeks after that, forty million acres were restored to the Navajo, more than twenty thousand acres to the Yakima, and sixty thousand acres to the Warm Springs Tribe in Oregon. And those were just the largest in a rapid succession of land settlements that favored the tribes.

Nixon's legislative initiative announced that July day added over $100 million to federal spending on behalf of Indians in every area, including education, housing, economic development, health care, and legal services. New programs were offered on behalf of urban Indians, replacing the yoke of Relocation. Specific programs offered nearly $1 million in new scholarships for Indian students, as well as double the amount of money to be spent on health in specific areas of combating alcoholism and drug abuse.

Termination was dead. The "Doomsday Book" could be thrown in the trash. Relocation was over. Later government statistics would show Termination had resulted in the movement of some two hundred thousand Indians, a migration from reservations on the scale of the Cherokees' Trail of Tears. Now tribes had the freedom to develop their own economic resources and employ their own people on their own land. It was the beginning of an entirely new era for Native Americans.

I hope you will understand that I mean it modestly when I say that a small part of that change came from my desperate dash up the gangplank of the *Monte Cristo*.

■

There are many spectacular and romantic views from the homes and apartments on the hills of San Francisco, each of them unique in its own way. There is still only one high rise above the San Francisco Marina, however, that is near enough to the waterfront to have a special close-up view of Alcatraz. It was the building where Tim Findley was summoned to talk with his editor about restoring the lighthouse beacon. Rich people live there. Many of them have enough time on their hands to appreciate truly the view from their patios. As the spring of 1971 began, a few of them kept their binoculars trained in sharp focus on the island. The government had given them a job to do in helping to keep track of the Indians coming and going from Alcatraz.

22

Removal

Y OU MIGHT SAY THE GOVERNMENT had some good reasons to begin losing patience with Alcatraz. President Nixon had gone further than any previous U.S. chief executive in recognizing and restoring the rights of Native Americans. Congress was following his lead with a swarm of new legislation that granted autonomy to the tribes while at the same time increasing the federal investment in assisting them. Everywhere you looked in the news media there seemed to be some account of either the new federal initiative or of Indians themselves taking action. The impression left was that there were more Indians in America than most people had realized, more everywhere. Except at Alcatraz.

John Trudell was realistically honest when he said that the occupation could support only very limited numbers of Indians living on the island. After the government removed the water barge and cut off power, and after the fires had done their damage, conditions were more bleak than ever. I think we were privately certain that the government would never go so far as to allow the siege to result in a serious health hazard to the occupiers. If, as Trudell and others had hinted at one point, a large number chose to hold out on the island in a success-or-suicide sort of stand like that of the Hebrews against the Romans at Masada, I think the government would have relented and restored basic services to the island. As it was, however, the actual population on Alcatraz became more transitory than ever. The boats made their regular runs to and from the mainland, and daylight hours would frequently find only a handful of Indians remaining on the island with almost nothing to occupy their time. From the distant verandas of the San Francisco high-rise the spotters silently watched and jotted down notes and numbers to be passed on to the FBI. Occasionally a white Coast Guard helicopter would slap low overhead, seemingly on its way out to some mission beyond the Golden Gate. The helicopter passes were frequent enough to begin to seem routine, incidental to the occupation; the crewmen on board were actually compiling a steady record from their surveillance photos. The government knew how few Indians actually still held the Rock.

Garment and Robertson still apparently held out some hope for a negotiated settlement that could calm the increasingly impatient hawks in the administration. They continued to set up talks with Trudell and La Nada and others that stressed the offer of an "Indianized" park on the island. But the occupiers held firm, realizing that the only strong card they held was the island itself. I think hope remained that despite what they also realized was dwindling interest and support, the longer they could hold on the better chances would be they would get some unforeseen help. The government's counter to that was the same carrot Robertson had held out before in the form of a $50,000 development grant now directed from the office of Governor Ronald Reagan to BANAC. It was suggested, for example, that part of the money might be used to begin restoration of the San Francisco Indian Center.

That sort of divide and conquer technique had its intended effect in spreading the mistrust between the mainland and what remained of Indians of All Tribes on Alcatraz. I had almost no part in the discussions by then. Squabbles over money had become increasingly petty and laced with suspicious accusations. Even a relatively minor $20 donation now became a fight over where to deposit the check.

I don't know where all the money went, or even how much of it there really was. Later, some others who had been on the island said they saw bags full of letters dumped on Richard's desk and emptied of all cash and checks before being tossed away, unread. But I don't think Richard made off with any large sum of money. He really was driven more by idealism and the narcotic of personal recognition than he was by greed. Money certainly found its way into unknown hands to pay for nights on the mainland or even trips back home. The bullying pressures employed during the worst period of no leadership undoubtedly worked for some in adding to their personal income. But I don't think anyone ever embezzled a lot of money from the occupation. Most of it was just frittered away, wasted in a lack of planning and direction.

On the night of April 19, 1971, the *Clearwater* mysteriously sank at her mooring alongside the island. It was another of those incidents like the fire about which we may never know the truth. Could government "frogmen" have sabotaged the boat as part of some covert exercise? Had someone just been neglectful in maintaining the overworked vessel? No one knew, but the fact was that the former fishing boat made possible by a donation from the rock group was the occupation's last reliable link to the mainland. There was not enough money to keep hiring private boats to run out people and supplies, and the days of generous, eager support from yachtsmen had long passed, spoiled in part by the hostility of the Indians on the island themselves.

Survival on Alcatraz, and survival of the occupation itself, now depended on even more desperate appeals for help. How much easier it might have been had we all just recognized how far we had come, how much we had actually achieved. But we did not. It would be simple and predictable to blame the divisions between us on the characteristic disputes that always seem to be part of Indian politics, whether between tribes or among individuals within the same cultural heritage. Tribal politics are notoriously fractured by dissension and personal resentment. But that really wasn't all of it, or even what I think was most of it. The government's games with offers to talk to one faction and put out money to another certainly played a part in it. Even more than that, however, were the times themselves. Vietnam, and then Cambodia and the widening war in general, hung like a backdrop curtain behind everything. Demonstrations for civil rights had melded into massive marches against the imperialism of federal policy. More and more, because of Vietnam especially, you were either for the government and the Nixon administration or against it. You couldn't just pick your particular issue, or at least within the intensely activist pressure of the Bay Area you couldn't, and expect that your cause would receive support that was apart from the agenda of others. The media's attention was on steadily more radical and more militant actions that signified a mood of resistance.

The defiant attitude of those in the occupation, including of La Nada and Trudell was, I think, as much a part of that trend as it was in any way a reasonable approach to winning the support they needed. Those of us in the mainland group were obviously more conservative in our continued approach to call attention to the urban Indian, but that seemed to have less and less to do with what could be accomplished on Alcatraz. Neither of our factions saw how we could consolidate our efforts and perhaps recover some of the advantage we had lost. Even with another summer break from college upon us, the support we needed just was no longer there.

The notation on Bud Krogh's memo of June 10, 1971, to John Ehrlichman, written by another staffer, read: "Bud: E agrees with you. Go!"

The last efforts of Garment, Patterson, and Bob Robertson's task force to come up with some settlement had failed. James Browning, the Republican appointee who had replaced a sympathetic but politically helpless Cecil Poole as U.S. attorney for the San Francisco district, was quoted in the

The coast guard ship with evacuated Indians and federal marshals. Photograph by Ilka Hartmann.

Chronicle as saying that "there is an increased possibility of violence by violence-prone individuals. I am hopeful of some way to avoid a confrontation, but if we have to have a showdown, we will have it." Privately, Browning had already decided that any further meetings with the Indians would be useless.

■

Krogh's memo to Ehrlichman recommended that "in spite of the risk of violence," a special force of U.S. marshals should be utilized to remove the Indians from Alcatraz. "Go!" came the response from Ehrlichman.[1]

By everyone's account, June 11 was a fine sun-basked day, unusual for that time of year on San Francisco Bay. Lazing around on a warm Friday afternoon, reporters at the city's daily newspapers were almost annoyed by the tips from waterfront sources that groups of heavily armed men were boarding a Coast Guard cutter for some kind of mission.

Krogh's tightly classified force of federal marshals and Coast Guard security had trained for weeks, trying to anticipate everything from armed

Exhausted and disillusioned, young Atha Rider WhiteManKiller, a Cherokee, speaks eloquently to the press, explaining that the purpose of the occupation was to broadcast his people's plight and establish a landbase for the Indians of the Bay Area. His words were the most quoted of the day. Photograph by Ilka Hartmann.

resistance (both onshore and off the island), to a wild mouse chase through the tunnels at the very depths of the Rock. They had been knit into a unique unit for this singular mission, and though most of them wore the bland suits and ties that fronted them as federal agents, they regarded what they had to do as a military action.

Delbert Lee, a twenty-two-year-old Sioux, was in one of the cottages he called his house, when a friend ran in, "and he tells me there's a bunch of reporters down on the dock with rifles."

A blinding-white eighty-two-foot Coast Guard cutter had slid into virtu-ally the identical landing alongside the dock that Peter Bowen and his *Sea-*

John Trudell speaks: "We were using the island as a means of reminding the government that Indian people got rights." Photograph by Ilka Hartmann.

weed had used to bring the first Indians ashore nineteen months earlier. Two other forty-foot Coast Guard craft were in at the slips. All of them were unloading suited men carrying semiautomatic weapons and shotguns. Before Lee could even look out to count them, a Coast Guard helicopter roared overhead and made a sharp turning pass back across the island.

"We were just doing craft work when someone hollered, 'There are people on the island with guns!'" remembered Atha Rider WhiteManKiller. "We ran down. There were federal marshals holding automatic weapons and shotguns, going through the buildings. They told us if we cooperated, we would not be handcuffed."

It was a total surprise. Even the media, tipped off by their sources on the waterfront, arrived too late to get past the gun-flashing perimeter quickly set up around the island by other Coast Guard boats.

There were fifteen Indians: six men, four women, and five children on the island. One more than had landed on November 9, 1969. None of them had been among the landing party then or in the invasion group of November 20. The media said they seemed confused when they were taken first to the military base at Yerba Buena Island, where they were questioned and fed lunch, and later when they were transported to San Francisco and given a night's lodging at a third-rate hotel in the Tenderloin.

That was it. The occupation was over. La Nada and John Trudell had both been off the island, trying to drum up more support, and their reactions were that it had been an obvious betrayal by the government of what they thought were continuing negotiations.

The real betrayal was only too obvious on Alcatraz itself. On the following Monday, federal authorities opened the island for a tour by newspeople that one described as being "more like an autopsy." The island we had hoped would be some kind of glittering symbol of Native American achievement was, in fact, a wreck. Glass windows in the most visible buildings had been shattered, allowing the cold and wet air to do its worst. Buildings were burned or partially dismantled for wood to burn elsewhere, and even the seemingly indestructible cell block seemed battered by blows to the concrete.

"Coiling along the narrow roads, looking like old skins shed by numerous snakes, were lengths of lead pipe dug up from utility tunnels, split and looted of their valuable copper tubing," reported the *San Francisco Chronicle*.

All those clothes, the toys for children, the general mess of donated items, were found by the touring media in what seemed to be windswept piles in the apartment buildings. The *Chronicle* reporter, Jerry Carroll, had been Tim Findley's best personal friend before Findley went on to work for *Rolling Stone*. It was, he knew, Tim's story to begin with, but he had to write the finale in the way he saw it:

"Another sign, sad and pathetic, is painted on a wall that looks yearningly out to the Bay Bridge: 'Where's our Chief?' it asks."

■

Officially, the occupation had lasted nineteen months and nine days. But nobody, not even the government, believed that was the end of it. All over the United States other occupations and demonstrations by American Indians continued for years, many of them led or drawing participants from the thousands of Indian people who had at some point passed through the island. AIM, never a part of the Alcatraz occupation itself, emerged as the strongly militant voice of Indian rights expressed in the pan-tribal way that Vine Deloria had once observed as missing from tribal arguments. AIM's holdout and exchange of gunfire with the FBI at Wounded Knee in 1975 would carry the movement beyond what had always been the nonviolent and unarmed character of the Alcatraz occupation, but the message of a new purposeful identity brought to Native Americans by Alcatraz was unmistakable. Not only Indians, but America itself, would never be the same. In that first year after removal of the last occupiers, I noted with some satisfaction that even American Indian art had almost doubled in value thanks in part to renewed interest in the Native American experience.

Richard Oakes's traveling university had, unfortunately, not gotten far before the old bus broke down. He was arrested outside Annie's Pomo reservation in Stewart's Point, California, for trying to impose a toll on motorists driving through the reservation. When federal agents removed the last of the occupiers, Richard called it a "sissy victory" and vowed to keep up the struggle on his own. I can't blame him for still being in search of that image he had found and lost on Alcatraz. Periodically he would still telephone Tim Findley (usually calling collect to Findley's home), to tell the reporter of yet another plan he had in mind. From undersea aquaculture he had gone on to a scheme of constructing high fences around properties to make deer ranches that would reintroduce a taste for venison in the United States. In a way seen later with buffalo ranches and even venison farms, Richard was ahead of his time; Tim always listened with a sympathetic but helpless ear to what he heard as Richard's attempt to restore his media reputation.

It was only a day or two after just such a phone call in September 1972 that Richard, still walking with a limp from the beating at Warren's, found himself in the middle of a dispute that involved Indian boys riding horses belonging to a YMCA camp in Mendocino County. I suppose that the camp authorities and their private security guards realized who Richard was and what potential trouble he might bring to them in siding with the Indian boys. They ordered him away from the property, but Richard refused to go for long. He still carried a reputation with him, but he was still alone. There was no occupation force or demonstration behind him, no threat I know of strong enough to cause the arming of YMCA camp guards. The guard there said he thought he saw Richard going for something in his coat. Without hesitating, the guard drew his 9mm pistol and shot Richard in the chest, killing him instantly. Although Richard had no weapon, a court later found that the guard had fired in self-defense. Richard Oakes was just thirty years old.

Findley's story was that sometime near dawn the next day, before he knew of what had happened to Richard, he was awakened by what he thought was someone calling his name. He looked out the window onto his deck with its commanding view of the Bay and saw a large black crow perched on the railing, seeming to stare at him before it lifted off and flew out across the Sausalito hills.

John Trudell, Richard's successor as the most recognized spokesman for the Alcatraz occupation, later became actively involved in the leadership of AIM and spent some time in Hollywood trying to start up a career in entertainment or broadcasting. Tragically, John's own family was killed in a fire at their home on a Paiute-Shoshone reservation in Nevada.

La Nada Boyer Means went on to earn her Ph.D. in sociology.

I have lost track of Al Miller and Joe Bill, but others tell me that they, too, returned to school and remained an important part of Native American affairs.

Jerry Hill, the former Los Angeles hairstylist who became a seeker on Alcatraz, was inspired by the experience to enter law school. He is now a lawyer and chief legal counsel for his own Oneida tribe near Greenbay, Wisconsin. "The really interesting thing was," Jerry said as he remembered the friends he made on the island, "that Vicki Santana became a lawyer even before I did." He had turned away from the island at last when he felt the occupation had gone out of control. And yet, regarding the decisions he made about his own life, he credited the experience on Alcatraz. "It led me home," he said.

Don Patterson became president of his own Tonkawa Tribe in Oklahoma, but he got his San Francisco Indian Center back before he left. After the occupation was ended, the government no longer saw a reason to keep dealing with BANAC, and those promises of money for urban Indian programs were never fulfilled. But with Dorothy Miller's help we raised over $7,000 to get a new Indian Center started, this time with its own retail outlet on the ground floor that helped finance its continued use in the same Mission District neighborhood.

I never did get back to my bowling and businessman style of life after Alcatraz. From the time the invasion planning began, I let my hair grow and have never cut it since. I was given the new name Fortunate Eagle by leaders of the Crow Nation in Montana, and by 1976 Bobbie, the kids, and I had moved from our home in San Leandro to her Shoshone reservation in Nevada.

Not that I ever forgot the spirit and the sometimes daring creativity that began it all. I still had my friends from the San Francisco Columbus Day Committee in mind in 1973 when I took a flight to Rome, and with paparazzi gathered all around me, stabbed my spear in the ground, claiming Italy for Native Americans by right of discovery. I had a meeting with the Pope himself after that and gave him a pipe as a token of my discovery.

Alcatraz itself did, of course, become part of the Golden Gate National Recreation Area, though never with the "Indian theme" that the government had promised. In 2001, the National Park Service for this area did release a statement focusing on the Indian occupation. My own contribution, and that of Richard Oakes, is described in this document as follows:

> While seemingly a mere media event, an unexpected result of this "Indian invasion" was a seed, an idea, which was planted in the minds of many Bay Area Indians, most importantly Adam (Nordwall) Fortunate Eagle and Richard Oakes. . . .
>
> Adam was a self-employed family man, quite active in the Bay Area Indian community. Richard was an idealistic college student at San Francisco State. Together they planned to take the Rock. . . .
>
> Adam was responsible for much of the behind the scenes planning and organization. He supplied the proclamation and the government needed a leader. The organization on and off Alcatraz didn't have a leader in the way that the media and the government understood. Richard was there to fill that role as well.
>
> But Richard and Adam were only two people in an occupation made up of thousands.

I am told that Alcatraz is now the second most-visited tourist attraction in the state of California, next only to Disneyland. People must book their visits there sometimes months in advance and pay a minimum of $5 for the ride out on tour boats that contract with the U.S. Park Service. Not a dime of it ever goes back to Indians who made it possible.

23

Renewal

SO THAT'S ONE STORY FROM THE BACK OF THE TURTLE. I know others have told the same story in their own way, and I hope Indian people especially will keep telling it forever.

Bobbie and I have a great-grandchild now, little Cienna. I will tell her the story as soon as she is old enough not to need a surrogate listener. Some of us, even now, may disagree about how and why things occurred the way they did around Alcatraz. The details of what happened may still divide us now and then. But it must always be known that, more than anything else, Alcatraz brought us together. It might seem strange to some in the future to imagine that we could have been unified and inspired by a bleak and inhospitable old prison that was used to punish and ruin so many other lives. They may find tragedy as well as triumph in our stories of what happened there.

You must remember that this story isn't really about Alcatraz at all. And like all really good stories, it has no real end.

Adam Fortunate Eagle in 1972. Photograph by Ilka Hartmann.

The Proclamation

We, the Native Americans, reclaim the land known as Alcatraz Island in the name of all American Indians by right of discovery. We wish to be fair and honorable in our dealings with the Caucasian inhabitants of this land, and hereby offer the following treaty:

We will purchase said Alcatraz Island for 24 dollars ($24) in glass beads and red cloth, a precedent set by the white man's purchase of a similar island about 300 years ago. We know that $24 in trade goods for these sixteen acres is more than was paid when Manhattan Island was sold, but we know that land values have risen over the years. Our offer of $1.24 per acre is greater than the 47 cents per acre the white men are now paying the California Indians for their land. We will give to the inhabitants of this land a portion of that land for their own, to be held in trust by the American Indian Government—for as long as the sun shall rise and the rivers go down to the sea—to be administered by the Bureau of Caucasian Affairs (BCA). We will further guide the inhabitants in the proper way of living. We will offer them our religion, our education, our life-ways, in order to help them achieve our level of civilization and thus raise them and all their white brothers up from their savage and unhappy state. We offer this treaty in good faith and wish to be fair and honorable in our dealings with all white men.

WE FEEL THAT THIS SO-CALLED ALCATRAZ ISLAND IS MORE THAN
SUITABLE AS AN INDIAN RESERVATION, AS DETERMINED BY THE WHITE
MAN'S OWN STANDARDS. BY THIS WE MEAN THAT THIS PLACE
RESEMBLES MOST INDIAN RESERVATIONS IN THAT:

1. It is isolated from modern facilities, and without adequate means of transportation.
2. It has no fresh running water.
3. The sanitation facilities are inadequate.
4. There are no oil or mineral rights.
5. There is no industry and so unemployment is very great.
6. There are no health care facilities.
7. The soil is rocky and nonproductive and the land does not support game.
8. There are no educational facilities.
9. The population has always been held as prisoners and kept dependent on others.

FURTHER, IT WOULD BE FITTING AND SYMBOLIC THAT SHIPS FROM
ALL OVER THE WORLD, ENTERING THE GOLDEN GATE, WOULD FIRST
SEE INDIAN LAND, AND THUS BE REMINDED OF THE TRUE HISTORY OF
THIS NATION. THIS TINY ISLAND WOULD BE A SYMBOL OF THE GREAT
LANDS ONCE RULED BY FREE AND NOBLE INDIANS.

USE TO BE MADE OF ALCATRAZ ISLAND

What use will we make of this land? Since the San Francisco Indian Center burned down, there is no place for Indians to assemble. Therefore, we plan to develop on this island several Indian institutions:

1. A Center for Native American Studies will be developed which will train our young people in the best of our native cultural arts and sciences, as well as educate them in the skills and knowledge to improve the lives and spirits of all Indian peoples. Attached to this Center will be traveling universities, managed by Indians, which will go to the Indian Reservations in order to learn from the people the traditional values which are now absent from the Caucasian higher educational system.
2. An American Indian Spiritual Center will be developed which will practice our ancient tribal religious ceremonies and medicine. Our cultural arts will be featured and our young people trained in music, dance, and medicine.
3. An Indian Center of Ecology will be built which will train and support our young people in scientific research and practice in order to restore

our lands and waters to their pure and natural state. We will seek to de-pollute the air and the water of the Bay Area. We will seek to restore fish and animal life, and to revitalize sea life which has been threatened by the white man's way. Facilities will be developed to desalt sea water for human use.

4. A Great Indian Training School will be developed to teach our peoples how to make a living in the world, improve our standards of living, and end hunger and unemployment among all our peoples. This training school will include a Center for Indian Arts and Crafts, and an Indian restaurant serving Native foods and training Indians in the culinary arts. This Center will display Indian arts and offer the Indian foods of all tribes to the public, so that all may know of the beauty and spirit of the traditional Indian ways.

5. Some of the present buildings will be taken over to develop an American Indian Museum, which will depict our Native foods and other cultural contributions we have given to all the world. Another part of the Museum will present some of the things the white man has given to the Indians, in return for the land and life he took: disease, alcohol, poverty and cultural decimation (as symbolized by old tin cans, barbed wire, rubber tires, plastic containers, etc.). Part of the Museum will remain a dungeon, to symbolize both those Indian captives who were incarcerated for challenging white authority, and those who were imprisoned on reservations. The Museum will show the noble and the tragic events of Indian history, including the broken treaties, the documentary of the Trail of Tears, the Massacre of Wounded Knee, as well as the victory over Yellow-Hair Custer and his Army. In the name of all Indians, therefore, we re-claim this island for our Indian nations, for all these reasons. We feel this claim is just and proper, and that this land should rightfully be granted to us for as long as the rivers shall run and the sun shall shine.

INDIANS OF ALL TRIBES
November, 1969
San Francisco, California

Notes

Chapter 2

1. Bob Robertson, "Alcatraz Closes," *San Francisco Chronicle*, March 22, 1963, p. 1.

2. Full accounts of this encounter were contained in several press reports of the time, the most complete of which was that of Jerry Martin, "War Dance on Alcatraz," *Oakland Tribune*, March 9, 1964, p. 1.

3. References to the 1868 Black Hills Treaty can be found in several publications, including Kappler, *Indian Affairs, Laws and Treaties*, vol. 2, 3rd ed. (Washington, D.C.: Government Printing Office, 1904). Many scholars and lawyers, including Vine Deloria, Jr., have examined the treaty and concluded it was not intended to offer up such "surplus" lands of the U.S. government. Nevertheless, the 1868 agreement is frequently cited in land disputes with Native Americans even today.

4. As reported in "Federal Reaction to Indian 'Invasion,'" *San Francisco Examiner*, March 9, 1964, p. 3.

Chapter 3

1. Joseph Jorgenson et al., *Native Americans and Energy Development* (Anthropology Resource Center, 1978), p. 24. See also Charles Lummis, *Bullying the Moqui* (Prescott, Ariz.: Prescott College Press, 1968); and Troy Johnson, *The Occupation of Alcatraz* (Urbana: University of Illinois Press, 1996).

2. See anonymous 1874 newspaper account of the Modoc War and Captain Jack at the Archivist, University of California–Berkeley and at the archives of the *San Francisco Chronicle*.

3. President Ronald Reagan address to Soviet students in Moscow, May 31, 1988, as reported in *San Francisco Examiner*, June 1, 1988, p. 3.

4. Thomas C. Leonard, "The Reluctant Conquerors," *American Heritage Magazine* (June 1970), p. 36. Custer eagerly published his views in 1874, two years before the Battle of the Little Bighorn: "If I were an Indian, I often think

I would greatly prefer to cast my lot among those of my people who adhered to the free open plains rather than submit to the confined limits of a reservation."

5. In addition to U.S. Census reports on demographics (various accounts), see also "A National Tragedy, A National Challenge," U.S. Senate Interior Subcommittee report on Indian Education, Ninety-first Congress, first session, 1969.

6. S. Lyman Tyler, "A History of Indian Policy," U.S. Department of the Interior, Bureau of Indian Affairs (1973), p. 154. See also Kenneth R. Philp, *John Collier's Crusade for Indian Reform* (Tucson: University of Arizona Press, 1977).

7. Ibid., with additional reference to Jorgenson, *Native Americans and Energy Development*.

8. La Nada (Boyer) Means's recollections of her childhood and younger years were first published in Peter Collier, "The Red Man's Burden," *Ramparts Magazine* (February, l970).

9. In her interview with Peter Collier, La Nada stated, "I took a lot of classes in subjects like 'laundry.'"

Chapter 4

1. For further reading on the Friendship House and the East Bay Native American community at the time, see Ilka Hartmann, "Indian in the City," *The Catholic Voice* 45 (March 15, 1973).

2. See also the essay by Ilka Hartmann, "Where Does the Indian Belong?" *Mill Valley Pacific Sun* (November 16, 1972), p. 11.

3. Tyler, "A History," p. 203. Quote taken from pamphlet titled "Answers to Your Questions about American Indians," U.S. Department of the Interior, Bureau of Indian Affairs (1973), pp. 18-23.

4. *St. Thomas Law Review* 10 (fall 1997), p. 75. See also Johnson, *Occupation of Alcatraz Island*.

5. Quoted to author by Mel Thom, director of Intertribal Friendship House, May 1967.

Chapter 5

1. California Assembly Joint Resolution No. 38, June 15, 1953.

2. The American Indian Movement first emerged with patrols of young Native Americans on the streets of Minneapolis in 1968 to counteract the "sweeps" of the so-called Red Ghetto by Minneapolis police. As reported in *Akwesasne Notes* (Minnesota) and other publications that year.

3. Story as told to author.

Chapter 6

1. One of the many problems created by the policy of Termination was that federal authorities lost track of where all the Indians were. Many of them seemed constantly in transit back and forth between the reservations and Relocation sites. This led to confusing statistics used both by the U.S. Department of the Interior and the new U.S. Department of Economic Opportunity, and the prob-

lem was noted in the Kennedy-Fannin hearings on poverty held by the U.S. Office of Economic Opportunity in 1968.

2. Transcript of John Plutte interview with Alan Miller, Golden Gate National Recreation Area (GGNRA), U.S. Park Service, 1996.

3. Lawrence Hauptmann, *White Roots of Peace, The Iroquois Struggle for Survival* (Syracuse, N. Y.: Syracuse University Press, 1968), p. 222.

4. See report and transcript of the "Public Forum Before the Committee on Urban Indians in San Francisco, California," April 11-12, 1969, produced by the National Council on Indian Opportunity.

5. Ibid., p. 54.

6. Ibid., p. 138.

7. Ibid., p. 243.

Chapter 7

1. Plutte interview with Al Miller.

Chapter 8

1. President Richard Nixon press statement and public release at the White House, September 27, 1968.

2. Walter Hickel address to the National Council on Indian Opportunity, Albuquerque, New Mexico, 1969.

3. Transcript of John Plutte interview with La Nada Means, GGNRA, U.S. Park Service, 1996.

4. The Proclamation written for delivery November 9, 1968.

Chapter 9

1. Plutte interview with La Nada Means.

2. Reconstructed from numerous later press accounts, including those taken from the *Chronicle* and from the *Examiner*. The author is grateful for the use, in this case and in others, of notes taken and saved by *Chronicle* reporter Tim Findley.

3. Plutte interview with La Nada Means.

4. Account provided by Tim Findley.

5. Plutte interview with La Nada Means.

6. Letter from R.Corbin Houchins to Dorothy "Lone Wolf" Miller, November 13, 1969.

Chapter 10

1. Transcript of John Plutte interview with Ed Castillo. GGNRA, U.S. Park Service.

2. While the author clearly could not have been present at these events, he is grateful for the extensive accounts provided to him by Tim Findley, Brooks Townes, Peter Bowen, and Mary Crowley, all of whom participated directly in the Alcatraz landing.

Chapter 11

1. Spiro Agnew speech to the National Congress of American Indians, October 8, 1969, Albuquerque, New Mexico.

2. This and other citations on the federal government's actions are taken from interviews conducted by the author with Bradley Patterson, and from Patterson's account offered in transcripts to the Golden Gate National Recreation Area, U.S. Park Service.

Chapter 12

1. Wire service accounts from *San Francisco Chronicle*, November 21, 1969, p. 1.

2. Plutte interview with La Nada Means.

3. Transcript of John Plutte interview of Shirley Guevara, GGNRA, U.S. Park Service.

Chapter 13

1. Transcripts of Plutte interviews, GGNRA, U.S. Park Service.

2. Interviews with Bradley Patterson confirmed the origin and use of this press release.

Chapter 17

1. Plutte interview with Al Miller.

2. Transcript of John Plutte interview with Vine Deloria, Jr., GGNRA, U.S. Park Service, 1996.

Chapter 18

1. As confirmed in recollections of Bradley Patterson.

2. Plutte interview with Al Miller.

Chapter 20

1. Transcript of John Plutte interview with John Trudell, GGNRA, U.S. Park Service, 1996.

Chapter 21

1. Richard Nixon address to Congress, July 8, 1970.

2. See R. C. Gordon, *The Taos Indians and the Battle for Blue Lake* (Red Crane Books, 1991). Also confirmed in written accounts of Bradley Patterson.

Chapter 22

1. Plutte interview with Bradley Patterson as confirmed in several conversations between the author and Patterson, and by letter from Patterson (1997) on his time serving as a White House aide.